TATHA WILEY

PAUL
AND THE
GENTILE WOMEN

Reframing Galatians

continuum

NEW YORK • LONDON

2005

The Continuum International Publishing Group Inc
15 East 26 Street, New York, NY 10010

The Continuum International Publishing Group Ltd
The Tower Building, 11 York Road, London SE1 7NX

Cover design: Sarah Rainwater

Cover art: Funerary Portrait of a Young Woman, ca. 161–180 CE. Encaustic on wood.
Location: Louvre, Paris, France.
Credit: Art Resource.

Printed in the United States of America

Library of Congress Cataloging-in-Publication Data

Wiley, Tatha.
    Paul and the gentile women : reframing Galatians / Tatha Wiley.
      p. cm.
    Includes bibliographical references and index.
    ISBN 0-8264-1706-X (hardcover : alk. paper) –
    ISBN 0-8264-1707-8 (pbk. : alk. paper)
    1. Bible. N.T. Galatians – Criticism, interpretation, etc. I. Title.

BS2685.52.W56 2005
227'.406 – dc22

2005002308

Continuum Publishing is committed to preserving ancient forests and natural resources. We have elected to print this title on 30% postconsumer waste recycled paper. As a result, this book has saved:

2.6 trees
125 lbs solid waste
1119 gallons of water
450 kw hours of electricity
242 lbs of net greenhouse gases

Continuum is a member of Green Press Initiative, a nonprofit program dedicated to supporting publishers in their efforts to reduce their use of fiber obtained from endangered forests. For more information, go to www.greenpressinitiative.org.

For
Nathan

Contents

PREFACE

P AUL'S LETTER TO THE GALATIANS draws us into the controverted heart of Christian origins. Situated in the diversity of Second Temple Judaism, Paul wrote to Gentile women and men in the Diaspora communities of Christ-followers he had founded. In Galatians, Paul vehemently rejects the position of fellow evangelists that circumcision be the sign of full membership in the eschatological covenant communities.

Galatians became a pivotal text for the subsequent tradition. The assumptions that Christians developed about Paul, his experience of the risen Christ, his mission to the Gentiles, his relation to Judaism, the meaning of the Jewish law, and the evangelists who challenged him dominated the reading of Galatians for a thousand years. At its center was Paul's contrast between "faith in Christ" and "works of the law." Used as short-hand for two religions, the phrases became ciphers for the superiority of Christian faith and the inferiority of Jewish Torah-observance. In subsequent eras, especially in the rallying cry of the Reformation, "justification by faith alone," Galatians became a battleground text, prized territory in momentous theological arguments among Christians over the role of faith, the nature of Christian conversion, the make-up of the Christian community, relations with the Jewish people, the worth of human beings, the character of authentic living, and ultimately the form of redemption itself.

Yet contemporary Pauline scholars have challenged virtually all of the historical and theological assumptions embedded
in the dominant interpretation of Galatians. A "new perspective" informs the reading of Galatians today, even among those
whose interpretation follows a different line of thought.[1] Both
presuppositions and conclusions are new. Exegetes and theologians once presumed, for example, that Paul's theological
concepts — such as justification — could be discussed independently of their social setting. Today it is axiomatic that meanings
are intimately bound up with social settings. While Paul's theology of justification is deeply rooted in the Jewish tradition,
his understanding cannot be separated from the struggle in
which he is engaged with other Jesus evangelists. What is to
be asked of these Gentiles drawn by his preaching of the risen
Christ? What is the means of their justification? Their faith in
Christ, Paul says, nothing more. His answer, taken for granted
by Christians for centuries, raised such concern among his fellow Jewish disciples of Jesus that some risked his certain fury to
come into assemblies he had established and to tell the believers
what the God of Israel required of them.

To say this much about the historical conflict reflects a significant shift in perspective from the tradition. To bring the
Gentile women into the center of this perspective further re-
frames our reading of Galatians and prompts a new flow of
questions.[2] What did circumcision signify for men? For women?
What obligations did it impose? What effect on the assembly
would its acceptance bring? What changes for the members?

These questions extend the "new perspective." Addressing
them results in a historical reconstruction that, if compelling,
fundamentally changes the way we think about Galatians.
Commentators have long noted the social function of the law as
a boundary marker for the people of Israel. But the boundaries

that the law marks are internal to the covenant community as well. In this work I will argue that the dispute between evangelists over the necessity of circumcision was, in its immediate communal context as well as direct consequence, a dispute over whether the membership of Gentile believers in the Galatian assemblies would be differentiated by gender.

The Galatian conflict was not a battle between two religions. Christianity as a distinct religion lay in the future. Paul's letter, the messianic movement in which he is engaged, the assemblies of Gentile believers, and the conflict with other Jesus disciples stood fully within the diversity of first-century Jewish life. This quarrel over what Gentiles must do was a Jewish fight. The competing theological positions were Jewish. The competitors were Jewish. The symbols of their worldview were Jewish. The Savior they proclaimed with one voice was Jewish.

Paul's fellow evangelists proposed a radical change in the assemblies Paul had established. To appreciate the nature of this change, we must inquire into how acceptance of the sign of circumcision would transform the existing assemblies and the relations among their members. Reframing Galatians also involves freeing the text from traditional miscues and resituating the text in light of a new analysis. Chapter 1 replaces the supersessionist reading of Galatians that has dominated the tradition with the insights of the "new perspective." Chapter 2 places Paul's religious call and mission in the context of the diversity of Second Temple Judaism and a still-Jewish messianic movement. Chapter 3 takes up the identity of Paul's opponents and the character of their struggle to win the hearts and minds of the Gentile women and men who were members of the Galatian assemblies. Chapter 4 focuses specifically on the situation of the Galatian women and their responses to the circumcision preaching, especially in the context of Jewish and Greco-Roman women in the ancient world. Chapter 5 raises the issue of why the question of the Gentile women has been largely absent from the exegetical tradition, where it leads us when the conceptualist and supersessionist readings of Galatians are properly abandoned, and what the struggle over circumcision meant for the very nature of these religious assemblies.[3]

My engagement with Galatians originates in teaching the New Testament and in exchanges with students and colleagues about the text and the historical situation to which it points. Work on this project precedes my historical and systematic study, *Original Sin*, and the edited volume in Christology, *Thinking of Christ*. It has been an absorbing and enriching interest. Happily, it has received encouragement and generated conversation. In particular, I would like to thank Barbara E. Bowe (Catholic Theological Union), Beverly Roberts Gaventa (Princeton Theological Seminary), K. C. Hanson (Fortress Press), Carolyn Osiek (Brite Divinity School), and Calvin Roetzel (Macalester College). An invitation from Carol J. Dempsey (University of Portland) and Mary Margaret Pazdan (Aquinas Institute of Theology) to present this project in the Feminist Biblical Hermeneutics Group at the Catholic Biblical Association was a source of valuable feedback. I am deeply grateful to Frank Oveis of Continuum Publishing for his warm welcome of this book and am honored to be among those who have worked with him in his distinguished career as editor.

I hope that readers find the questions generating this study engaging and the reconstruction of the historical circumstances addressed in Paul's letter plausible. Reframing Galatians in this way offers renewed reason to reflect on its striking pertinence to today's Christian community and the redemptive witness it bears to women and men.

Chapter One

GALATIAN DISPUTES

=====

INTERPRETED SO OFTEN BY SO MANY, Paul's Letter to the Galatians would seem to have little more to yield. Yet sometimes new questions disclose previously unnoticed dimensions of a text, and meanings long taken for granted can be transformed by new methods of inquiry. New insights in biblical studies reconfigure interpretive expectations and assumptions. In fact, the historical realities explained by new interpretations may be quite different from those supposed by commentators throughout the tradition. Such reinterpretation was the contribution of twentieth-century studies of the Apostle Paul. The results constitute a genuinely "new perspective" within which Galatians is now interpreted.[1]

Interpreting Galatians requires negotiating an exegetical tradition steeped in technical literary and historical analyses, competing theological viewpoints, Christian theological anti-Semitism, and the rich nuances of Paul's theological horizon. Yet however concise the analyses, cogent the judgments, and impressive the perspective, interpretations are finite. There are always further questions to be posed to a classic. We must also bear in mind, James Dunn writes, "the possibility or indeed likelihood that the situations confronting Paul were more complex than we can now be aware of, or include important aspects which are now invisible to us." In the case of Galatians, particularly, some fail "to grasp the full significance of *the social function of the law* at the time of Paul and how that determines and influences both the issues confronting Paul and Paul's responses."[2]

Much has been written about the function of the Jewish Torah in its civil role as constitution and its social role as marker of the boundary between covenant insider and outsider. Yet in the analysis of Galatians, little attention has been given to the social function of the law in creating boundaries between covenant insiders themselves.[3] Without attending to this internal function of the law, the full impact of the conflict over circumcision and works of the law is missed. Acceptance or rejection of the Torah as the norm for living bears directly on the social reality of the Galatian assemblies. As an ordering principle for gender relations, the Torah's acceptance would be decisive.

The Jewish sect Paul joined already included women as participants and leaders.[4] Prisca, for example, is acknowledged by the title *synergos*, a "co-worker" or missionary like Paul himself. But she is independent of him and not under his authority.[5] Paul's references to "brothers," and his other masculine terms, might have us think he was writing only to males. As Calvin Roetzel notes, however, Paul uses the term *sons* "to refer to both female and male heirs of God's promise (3:28–29)," among whom were "a number of female leaders on whom he lavishes praise."[6] Paul's ministry continued the social radicalism embodied in Jesus' followers and the early Christian movement. His proclamation of "freedom in Christ" (5:1) placed liberation from unjust structures and relations at the heart of the experience of redemption.[7] Women as well as men were drawn to his offer of Christ's salvation.

The gender-inclusive character of the Diaspora communities is routinely noted by Pauline scholars in conjunction with the baptismal confession Paul cites: "There is no longer Jew or Greek, there is no longer slave or free, there is no longer male and female, for all of you are one in Christ Jesus" (3:28). Scholars may advert to the difference between the *or* in the first two pairs and the *and* in the third pair. But consideration of gender is often — not always — left there, with commentators turning their focus to other aspects of the text.[8] While the subject of Paul and women has produced its own mountain of literature, the impact of the appropriation of the sign of circumcision on the actual members of these assemblies — especially on the Gentile women — remains a question unposed by scholars. Why would the circumcision preaching be of consequence for women? I will argue that Paul's opponents' position threatened the redemptive equality symbolized by baptism and made real by its performance. The circumcision preaching bears directly on gender, and gender is at the heart of the Galatian conflict.

A VOLATILE MIX

The historical situation reflected in Paul's Letter to the Galatians was a volatile mix, with competing evangelists citing different scriptural warrants and urging different conditions for Gentile inclusion in the people of Israel. Women and men who had joined the charismatic assemblies founded by Paul, professing belief in the God of Israel and Jesus as Lord, were now caught between two visions of how these communities were to be constituted.

This dispute consumed Paul's attention in Galatians. It centered first on scripture. Was God's command to Abraham that circumcision be the sign of covenant membership still normative?[9] The answer that scripture itself provides is definitive: "Any uncircumcised male who is not circumcised in the flesh of his foreskin shall be cut off from his people; he has broken my covenant" (Gen. 17:14).

Like Paul, the evangelists opposing him were Jewish followers of Jesus, for whom the scripture was authoritative and revelatory. Unlike Paul, they understood the law as having a new function in the affairs of ordinary life and for salvation. Their gospel, Carolyn Osiek writes, "assumed that people's access to Christ required that they obey the Mosaic law, or at least some of its major requirements, including circumcision."[10] The law had always been a *means*, not an end in itself; but now, with the resurrection of Jesus ushering in the eschatological age, its function within the covenant became the means to Christ's salvation. For many Jews who became Jesus-followers, like these evangelists, faith in Christ did not replace the Torah but completed it. They understood the Christ-event through the prevailing Jewish theology, the cardinal elements of which E. P. Sanders highlights: "Belief that their God was the only true God, that he had chosen them and had given them his law, and that they were required to obey it are basic to Jewish theology, and they are found in all sources."[11]

Galatians affords us a glimpse into the diversity among the earliest Jewish Jesus-followers in their understanding of the relation of the risen Christ to the Torah. Some did not find faith in Jesus as glorified Lord incompatible with continued Torah-observance. As Larry Hurtado emphasizes:

Some Jewish Christians (the "circumcision party") demanded that Gentile believers, in addition to putting faith in Jesus also take up full observance of Torah. Otherwise they had not made a full conversion to the God of Israel.... They could be treated as members of the Jewish

people only if they made a proper conversion that involved
a commitment to observance of Torah (e.g., Sabbath, food
laws, and for males, circumcision).[12]

For those evangelists actively "correcting" Paul's position in
Galatia, God's command to Abraham remained as absolute as
before. If Gentiles wanted to share in Israel's biblical promises,
they had to do what God had demanded of Israel. Galatian
women and men were to enter into Israel in the same way as
Gentile converts were generally expected to come. The normal
way for males was by the ritual of circumcision. A ritual of
immersion constituted the normal way for females. For both
women and men, the rituals of initiation obligated them to
live the way of the Torah in their subsequent lives. They were
now Jews.

Against this formidable position, Paul argued from his own
experience and that of the Gentile women and men to whom
he writes. The "truth of the gospel" was God's acceptance
of outsiders — validated through gifts of the Spirit — into
Israel's covenant as the women and men they were (2:5; 2:14–
16).[13] Those persons drawn to Christ through Paul entered
into the Jesus community in the same way as he had, by religious conversion. Immersion confirmed their commitment to
the God of Jesus. It grounded the restoration of equality:
"You are one in Christ Jesus" (3:28).[14] Privilege was conspic-
uously absent from the social reality of their communities.
For women, freedom from subordinate status was intrinsic to
the experience of redemption. As Krister Stendahl long ago
noted, "Through baptism a new unity is created, and that is
not only a matter discerned by the eyes of faith but one that
manifests itself in the social dimensions of the church (Gal.
2:11–14)."[15]

New Perspective and Beyond

The conclusions of contemporary Pauline scholars stand in stark contrast to traditional interpretation. Throughout the Christian tradition, the circumcision preaching had been interpreted as a threat not to the equality of members in the assemblies but to the legitimacy of the Christian gospel. Christian commentators took Paul's heated opposition to the law as a sign that Judaism represented an inferior spirituality of works-righteousness. With the acceptance of circumcision, Torah-observance would once again separate covenant insiders from outsiders. Further, these exegetical conclusions informed a whole theology and anthropology deeply influential in Christian history, often supersessionist in content, vindictive in tone.

Reframing Galatians today therefore takes place against the backdrop of (1) recent dethroning of a centuries-old exegetical consensus about the historical circumstances of the letter, (2) use of the letter in bitter and divisive feuds over crucial theological issues, and (3) the letter's role in a long and shameful history of Christian supersessionism. This work attempts to sort through that complex legacy, appropriate the insights of the new perspective, and move beyond them to a new and theologically more promising reconstruction.

Twentieth-century studies brought into sharper relief the Jewish character of the messianic movement that Paul had first opposed and then embraced. A deeper grasp of the diversity of Second Temple Judaism yielded the discovery that Jews debated the question of Gentile conversion, and views varied widely among them.[16] As a Jewish disagreement, the Galatian dispute between messianic evangelists was not unique. Even the basic element of Paul's position — acceptance of Gentile men without circumcision — was not unheard of in Diaspora Judaism.[17]

Salvation of the "righteous Gentile" was a topic of debate in Philo, 2 Baruch, and elsewhere.[18] Scholars acknowledged the Jewishness of the Galatian dispute as well as the Jewishness of the alternatives posed. Some can even acknowledge the reasonableness of the other evangelists' position.[19] Thus, except in the most conservative circles, the work of such figures as E. P. Sanders, James D. G. Dunn, and Alan Segal has decisively turned scholarly attention to the difference these positions made for membership in the assembly.[20]

But this judgment — that the Galatian fight was over *membership* — precipitates a flood of further questions. How would women believers have heard the message of the other evangelists and interpreted their arrival? Why would men have been attracted to Paul's challengers? How would women have heard Paul's letter? And men? How would a Torah-observant community differ from the present charismatic assembly?[21]

In Peter Lampe's judgment, we already know something of the social reality of these communities through their baptismal confession. While men and women were Jew or Gentile, slave or free, male or female outside the community, these distinctions did not hold in the "new creation" of the Christian community. The norms of the ancient world did not control relations in the *ekklēsia* or Christian assembly. Here no one was privileged. "In Galatians 3:28 Paul states that whatever the worldly differences among the Galatians may be, they are abolished."[22] This radical equality — of religion, class, gender — was embodied in the participation of members in the community and in shared leadership roles. Lampe argues that the evidence is such that we can assume that the equality of all congregational members was "part of the constructed social reality of the first Christian generation — at least in the Pauline churches."[23] Elisabeth Schüssler Fiorenza points to the significance of their common initiation ritual. "If it was no longer circumcision but baptism which was the primary rite of initiation, then women became full members of the people of God with the same rights and duties."[24] Schüssler Fiorenza's comment invites further reflection about the dynamics of the Galatian situation. What did the positions of Paul and the other evangelists on circumcision say about who was to be a full member of the assembly?

Why did these evangelists preach to the Galatian believers? Paul's challengers did not come to oppose unrestricted social interaction between Jews and Gentiles. Unlike in Antioch, these assemblies are thought to be exclusively Gentile.[25] Nor does evidence suggest that the issue was food. As many have argued, they came to challenge Paul's understanding of the conditions of Gentile membership in the people of God. Asking how the already-present Gentile inclusion would be changed by accepting circumcision and works of the law, I will argue that the purpose of the other evangelists' coming is consistent with the gendered sign of membership they advocate.

The Use and Abuse of Paul

Since this inquiry directly involves reconstructing the conflictive situation in which Paul's inclusion of Gentile women and men in the people of God had placed them, it is also crucial to see and sort through clearly the past ideological use of the letter and its relation to our question. Responsible interpretation of the letter today must bear the supersessionist exegetical heritage of Galatians in mind.

We come to Galatians deeply influenced by this tradition. The text has been accompanied by derogatory depictions of Jews, the announcement of God's abandonment of Israel, and the proclamation of Christianity as Israel's covenant replacement.[26] As noted, at the center of Christian supersessionism was the contrast Paul drew in Galatians between "works of the law" and "faith in Christ" (2:16). His contrast was taken as an indictment of an inferior religion based on works and an affirmation of a superior religion based on faith. The "truth" of this exegesis went unquestioned until the twentieth century.

The horrific events of World War II exposed the human tragedy that issues from ground prepared by religious invective. The stark evil of the *Shoah* unmasked the unreflective contempt for Jews embedded in Christian worship and thought. Christian theology faced a fundamental challenge. After Auschwitz, "it is not a matter of a revision of Christian theology with regard to Judaism," Johann-Baptist Metz wrote, "but a matter of the revision of Christian theology itself."[27]

Outright rejection of the Christian *adversus Judaeos* tradition proved difficult. Anti-Judaism is not a separate text that can be expunged, repented, and forgotten. It is embedded throughout the work of early Christian writers — in their homilies and prayers and in their christologies, soteriologies, and ecclesiologies. Christian supersessionism seemed straight from God via Paul's harsh words about the law and about those who argued its necessity. For Christians through the centuries, Paul's letters have been a source of spiritual insight. But appropriated by writers in the *adversus Judaeos* tradition, they contributed as well to a deep and abiding spiritual blindness. Jewish scholar Daniel Boyarin writes that:

> much of the horror inflicted on the Jews in this century can be traced at least partially to theologically informed attitudes of contempt for Jews. These attitudes of contempt are partially produced in the context of a particular

reading of Paul's texts, a reading which depicts him attacking Judaism as an inferior, mechanistic, commercialized religion.[28]

After Auschwitz, however, Pauline scholarship dealt with a new question: Was Paul the origin of Christian theological anti-Semitism? Pauline studies became part of an intensive post–World War II endeavor to determine the roots of Christian theological anti-Semitism and the reason for its development. Exegetical interpretations of Galatians today reflect a concerted effort to understand Paul in the historical context of first-century Judaism. Unlike the abstract and theological interpretation of the prior tradition, interpretation today is concrete and social. Phrases such as "works of the law" and ideas such as resurrection are found to mean something considerably different than the meanings attributed to them in the Christian tradition.[29]

Christian writers in the church's first centuries found it difficult to appreciate, in E. P. Sanders's words, that Paul's opponents brought to Galatia "an entirely reasonable position."[30] Several factors created obstacles to granting the integrity of these evangelists' argument.

One obstacle was misunderstanding of the issue of circumcision itself. The insistence on circumcision looks quite different if it is presumed, as the patristic writers did, that Paul had converted to a new religion, Christianity, and rejected the old one, Judaism.[31] Paul's harsh words about the law, perhaps especially his dismissive references to "works of the law," were taken as reasons for rejecting Judaism. His repeated comment in Galatians that justification is through faith in Christ "and not by doing the works of the law, because no one is justified by the works of the law" (2:16) seemed unambiguous. Believing in Christ is superior to Torah-observance. Paul's original point was that Gentile women and men no longer needed to adopt the Jewish way of life for inclusion in Israel's covenant, but the early church theologians took him to mean that the law itself was no longer valid.[32] The *adversus Judaeos* tradition set a superior Christianity (faith) over against an inferior Judaism (law).

A further obstacle was taking Paul's polemical caricature of his opponents as an accurate depiction of historical reality.[33] Paul throws out a barrage of hostile remarks against the evangelists challenging him, splicing his letter with direct and indirect indictments. His opponents are confusing Paul's Gentile converts (1:7; 5:10) and perverting the gospel (1:7). They should be cursed for proclaiming a gospel contrary to Paul's (1:8–9). Their gospel, unlike Paul's, is of human origin (1:11). They think (mistakenly) that justification comes through doing works of the law (2:15). They are bewitching the Galatian men and women (3:1). Those who rely on the law are under a curse (3:10). They want to make women and men subject to the law (4:21). They want to submit the Gentile believers to the yoke of slavery (5:1). They are preventing Paul's converts from obeying the truth (5:7). Even they do not obey the law (6:13). Paul wishes that the ones who "unsettle you would castrate themselves" (5:12). Coupled with the persuasiveness of Paul's rhetoric, the real-life hostility of the patristic theologians for Jews blocked a sympathetic reading of Paul's opponents' position.

The polemical language Paul uses so effectively reflects genuine differences among Jews about Gentile conversion. Similarly, in the gospels, hostile language about "the Jews" comes from Jews. This, too, reflects an intra-Jewish disagreement about the claims of Jewish messianists. The gospel writers place this later conflict back into the life of Jesus.

In the Gospel of Matthew, for example, "the Jews" are hypocritical in their worship and prayer (Mt. 6:2, 5, 16). They are an evil and adulterous generation (12:38, 45). They have evil in their hearts (9:4). The scribes have no authority (7:29). Jesus predicts his disciples will be flogged in synagogues (10:17). The Pharisees accuse Jesus of doing exorcisms by the power of the devil (9:34; 12:24) and conspire to destroy him (12:14). They, too, are hypocrites (15:6). The Pharisees and Sadducees test him (16:1). Before Pilate the crowd of Jews invite their own damnation: "Then the people as a whole answered, 'His blood be on us and our children!'"(27:25).

The Gospel of Matthew became the most favored of what became the four canonical gospels for use in liturgy, perhaps because of the erroneous assumption of its historical priority.[34] The context of these polemical references to the Jews was lost. They were heard simply as historical descriptions, depicting what the Jews were "really like." With the other gospels, perhaps more so given its liturgical use, Matthew shaped Christian consciousness of the Jews and Jesus' interaction with his contemporaries. The whole matter of redemption was seen to turn on the replacement of Jews by Christians, and not, as it had been for Jesus, on the in-breaking of the compassion of God in Jesus' ministry and the social transformation that could come with its appropriation.

Likewise, patristic theologians read Paul as repudiating Judaism and the Torah. They took his harsh words as revelation that the validity of the law ended with the advent of Christ (3:19–20). By the "truth of the gospel," Paul in fact meant that Gentiles were now accepted by God as Gentiles. To belong to Israel's covenant, they were no longer obliged to become Jews or accept Torah-observance. But early church theologians took the "truth of the gospel" to denote the replacement of the Jews by Christians in the covenant relationship with God. In his fourth-century *Catechetical Lectures*, Cyril of Jerusalem defined the church in this way, J. N. D. Kelly writes, as "a spiritual society which God called into existence to replace the Jewish church, which conspired against the Savior."[35] This assertion of replacement lies at the core of the *adversus Judaeos* tradition.[36]

Christians appropriated for themselves Israel's theologies of election and covenant. For Jews, the response to their election by God and the means of covenant fidelity was observance of the law God had given them. The Torah was the norm by which righteousness and sin were judged. For Christians the criterion for righteousness and overcoming sin became belief in Jesus Christ. Paul's defense of faith as the means for right relation to God was a foundational text: "a person is justified not by the works of the law but through faith in Christ" (2:16).

The author of Acts made the universal and absolute dimensions of the Christian proclamation clear: "And there is salvation in no one else, for there is no other name under heaven given among men by which we must be saved" (Acts 4:12). This Christocentric approach reversed Israel's theology of salvation. Now it was Gentiles — believers in Christ — who were in right relation to God, not Jews. Jews, not Gentiles, were now sinners. By their unbelief, writer after writer will assert, Jews put themselves outside the circle of righteousness.

For Israel, observance of the Torah separated the covenant community from the impurity of outsiders, just as a fence separates land. Paul's image of the "body of Christ" supplied for Gentiles an image analogous to the way the Torah functioned for Israel (1 Cor. 12:27; Rom. 12:5). In the Body of Christ believers are separated from outsiders who are nonbelievers. Israel's ethnocentrism became Christianity's Christocentrism.

At the heart of the proclamation of the later patristic theologians was their assertion that there is one mediator of salvation, Christ. Along with the text of Acts 4:12 and Acts 2:21 ("everyone who calls on the name of the Lord shall be saved"), Paul served as a basis for such a claim. In his Letter to the Romans, Paul wrote that "if you confess with your lips that Jesus is Lord and believe in your heart that God raised him from the dead, you will be saved" (Rom. 10:9). Paul retained the correlation between belonging to the covenant and salvation.[37] Being in the covenant was salvation. For Gentiles, belonging would be contingent on their faith in Christ.

The exclusivism with which Christ was preached was rooted in the patristic assumption that there can be only one true divine revelation and one authentic way of salvation. If Christ is this revelation and salvation, then the claims of other religions — namely, that they, too, possessed divine truth and salvific value — must be false.

This rejection of other religions was even more complete. If Christianity is true, early church theologians argued, then other religions are false. If they are false, there is only one religion. Exclusivist expressions accommodate the empirical fact of religious pluralism by drawing on the images of a hierarchy of religions or a fullness of truth. Christianity is the highest religion, for example, or possesses the fullness of divine truth.

The development of the doctrine of original sin in the church's first four centuries anchored Christian exclusivism deep in the soul. The doctrine first developed as a response to the question of why Christ's forgiveness is necessary for everyone. The gradual consensus was that everyone inherits a sin that requires forgiveness. The doctrine then has to do primarily not with the origin of sin but with the exclusive means of salvation. Because each person inherits the sin of Adam and Eve, each is in need of Christ's grace of forgiveness for salvation. The doctrine then links redemption with the church. Christ's forgiveness is mediated sacramentally through the baptism offered only by the church.[38] With official acceptance of the doctrine of original sin as church teaching, salvation was restricted — at least in the minds of early church theologians — to Christianity. Early disputes over Christian participation in the Jewish covenant had become transformed into reasons why the Jewish covenant was no longer valid and the Christian church held a monopoly on salvation.

For the patristic writers, the central issue was *identity*. How are Christianity and Judaism related? Their answers took on a formulaic character, asserting that Christ had replaced Moses, the Gospel had replaced the Torah, the church had replaced the synagogue, and so on. This ecclesial dimension of Christian exclusivism was made a theological principle by Cyprian in the third century: "Outside the church, there is no salvation."[39] This theological principle remained in place in the Roman Catholic Church until the Second Vatican Council. Protestants put the assertion in a Christocentric form: "Outside Christ, there is no salvation." Karl Barth, one of the most notable of twentieth-century Protestant theologians and deeply steeped in Paul, especially his Letter to the Romans, expressed the core of his theological perspective in a way that could have been the statement of any of the patristic writers: "God's true revelation is given to Christianity. There is one Savior, Jesus; one true religion, Christianity; one means of salvation, the church."[40]

Through the centuries, the Galatian legacy continued. The Christian gospel was not good news for Jews. Once Christianity became the religion of the empire under Constantine in the fourth century, the religious accusations of deicide and divine rejection of Jews justified denial of their social, political, economic, and religious rights, resulting in their marginalization and persecution.[41] A stock fund of hostile terms and images devaluing the Jews developed. These words and images could incite the violence against the Jews seen in medieval and modern pograms. Paul's "truth of the gospel" became a religious ideology of superiority justifying Christians as God's favored ones and denigrating Jews as those whom God has rejected.

Early Christian writers portrayed Jews in the darkest light. In his "Homily on the Passover," the second-century Melito of Sardis was the first to level the charge of deicide — killing God — against the Jews:

> O wicked Israel, why did you carry out this fresh deed of injustice, bringing new sufferings upon your Lord — your master, your creator, your maker, the one who honored you, who called you Israel? But you were discovered not to be Israel, for you have not seen God or acknowledged the Lord. . . .
>
> I am ashamed to say and compelled to speak. . . . Who was it? It is a heavy thing to say, and a most fearful thing to refrain from saying. But listen, as you tremble in the face of him on whose account the earth trembled. He who hung the earth in place is hanged. He who fixed the heavens in place is fixed in place. He who made all things fast is made fast on the tree. The Master is insulted. *God is murdered.* The King of Israel is murdered by an Israelite hand.[42]

Melito's charge is staggering. But the language used of the Jews by the fourth-century John Chrysostom, Bishop of Constantinople and one of the church's great commentators on scripture, is even more shocking:

Do not be surprised if I have called the Jews wretched and miserable for they have received many good things from God yet they have spurned them and violently cast them away. The sun of righteousness rose on them first, but they turned their back on its beams and sat in darkness. But we, who were nurtured in darkness, welcomed the light and we were freed from the yoke of error. The Jews were branches of the holy root, but they were lopped off. We were not part of the root, yet we have produced the fruits of piety. They read the prophets from ancient times, yet they crucified the one spoken of by the prophets.... They were called to sonship, but they degenerated to the level of dogs.... What sort of folly, what kind of madness, to participate in festivals of those who are dishonored, abandoned by God and provoked the Lord.... They killed the son of your Lord, and you dare to gather with them in the same place?[43]

A thousand years later, Martin Luther's answer to the question he posed to the German princes, about what to do with the Jews, is eerily evocative for its tragic parallel to actual twentieth-century events. His violent language reveals the spiritual blindness created by misreading of scripture and the subsequent development of the *adversus Judaeos* tradition:

What then shall we Christians do with this damned, rejected race of Jews? Since they live among us and we know about their lying and blasphemy and cursing, we cannot tolerate them if we do not wish to share in their lies, curses, and blasphemy.... First, their synagogues... should be set on fire, and whatever does not burn up should be covered over with dirt so that no one may ever see a cinder or stone of it.... Secondly, their homes should

likewise be broken down and destroyed. For they perpetu-
ate the same things there that they do in their synagogues.
For this reason they ought to be put under one roof or in
a stable, like gypsies, in order that they may realize that
they are not masters in our land, as they boast, but miserable captives.... Thirdly, they should be deprived of their
prayer books and Talmuds in which such idolatry, lies,
cursing, and blasphemy are taught. Fourthly, their rabbis
must be forbidden under threat of death to teach anymore.
Fifthly, passport and traveling privileges should be abso-
lutely forbidden to the Jews. For they have no business
in the rural districts since they are not nobles, nor offi-
cials, nor merchants, nor the like. Let them stay at home.
Sixthly, they ought to be stopped from usury. All their cash
and valuables of silver and gold ought to be taken from
them. Everything that they possess they stole and robbed
from us through their usury, for they have no other means
of support....

To sum up, dear princes and nobles who have Jews in
your domain, if this advice does not suit you, then find a
better one so that you may all be free of this insufferable
devilish burden — the Jews.[44]

The sin of the Jews lay in their failure to acknowledge Jesus
as Messiah in the first century and refusal to convert to Christianity in the centuries that followed. Until removed from the
liturgy by Pope John XXIII in 1959, this Good Friday Prayer
was heard annually by Catholics worldwide:

Let us pray also for the unfaithful Jews, that our God and
Lord may remove the veil from their hearts; that they also
may acknowledge our Lord Jesus Christ. Almighty and
everlasting God, Who drivest not even the faithless Jews

away from Thy mercy, hear our prayers, which we offer
for the blindness of that people, that, acknowledging the
light of thy truth, which is Christ, they may be rescued
from their darkness.[45]

Rooted in the religious privilege assumed by the early Christians, the *adversus Judaeos* tradition ignored the redemptive
insights of the scriptures themselves — the prophetic call for
justice and compassion for the vulnerable, Jesus' *basileia* vision
of inclusion and compassion for the other, and the baptismal
identification of religious privilege as sin.

Against this background, the achievement of post–World
War II Pauline scholarship can be gauged. It has transformed
the inherited theological interpretation of Paul. In his 1977
work *Paul and Palestinian Judaism*, E. P. Sanders described a
primary purpose of his work as overcoming the depiction of Judaism as a legalistic religion. He argued that the work of earlier
scholars was based on a massive perversion and misunderstanding of Judaism in the first century and the development of
Rabbinic Judaism after the destruction of the Temple and Jerusalem in 70 C.E. and following.[46] Today prominent Pauline
scholars such as Sanders reject the idea that a theology of works-
righteousness can be found at all in Second Temple Judaism.[47]
It is a polemical caricature of Judaism, not historical reality.

The "paradigm shift" Sanders engendered in Pauline studies
was a "gigantic breakthrough," as Jewish scholar Daniel Boyarin
emphasizes in remarking on the significance of Sanders's work.
Boyarin points to the crucial methodological shift that Sanders's
work has effected:

Sanders has forever changed the way Paul will be read
by scholars and interpreters of his work. In his mas-
terwork, he finally achieved what several Christian and

Jewish scholars (including Davies) had tried for decades
to achieve — to demonstrate that the slander of early Judaism promulgated by interpreters of Paul was simply and
finally just that, a slander. Pauline studies will never be the
same.... He has accomplished a gigantic breakthrough,
which, I think, will never be reversed: He demonstrated
that descriptions of the Judaism against which Paul is al-
legedly reacting *must be based first and foremost in realistic
and accurate descriptions of actually known Judaism and cannot be simply "reconstructed" from the Pauline texts themselves.*
Let me repeat the point: Whatever any interpreter ends
up saying about Paul and Judaism from now on starts from
actual Jewish texts and not from Paul.[48]

Two exegetical insights have been pivotal in transforming
the traditional reading of Paul. The first was into the nature of
Paul's "conversion." Paul's experience of the risen Christ generated a crossover from one Judaism to another, not a change
from one religion to another. The second insight was into the
nature of Paul's hostile language about the law. The validity
and value of the law *for Jews* was not the issue. At issue was
the necessity *for Gentiles* to appropriate a Jewish way of living.[49]
Paul's opponents linked salvation with covenant membership, as
did he; but they also continued to affirm — with scripture —
the necessity of Torah-observance for covenant fidelity, which
he did not. Paul separated salvation from Jewish nationalistic
identity.[50] At the heart of Paul's theology was the conviction,
as E. P. Sanders writes, "that Jesus Christ is Lord, that in him
God has provided for the salvation of all who believe (in the
general sense of 'be converted')...."[51] This first position is cap-
tured by the confession in Romans to which we have already
alluded: "If you confess with your lips that Jesus is Lord and

believe in your heart that God raised him from the dead, you shall be saved" (Rom. 10:9). Paul grounds the equality of Jews and Gentiles in their faith in Christ: "for in Christ Jesus you are all children of God through faith" (Gal. 3:26).[52] To recover the convictions underlying Paul's position, we turn next to his context.

Chapter Two

PAUL'S CONTEXT

O F THE WOMEN AND MEN first to proclaim Jesus as mediator of God's salvation, Paul undoubtedly became the
most influential for the subsequent tradition. His theological
axiom of justification by faith is as closely identified with Christian faith as any saying of Jesus. His dramatic experience of
the risen Christ is as familiar a story as that of Jesus' baptism
by John. Yet historical studies now make clear that assuming
the existence of "Christianity" in Paul's time is anachronistic.
Even the Rabbinic Judaism that Christians have imagined Paul
left to join Christianity is a second-century development. Dieter Georgi points out that the terms *Christian* and *Christianity*
are not Paul's. Paul "does not use the terms because he does
not know them."[1] No doubt, Paul's proclamation of God's acceptance of non-Jews contributed to developments eventually
transforming this Jewish messianic sect, of which he is a part,
into a distinct religion.[2] Granted, too, that what Paul says and
does will contribute to a parting of the ways yet ahead. But what
Paul proclaims he proclaims as a Jew. Developments yet ahead
are unknown to him. Recovering Paul's actual Jewish context has
been a major contribution of contemporary Pauline scholarship
and a key to his stance in Galatia.

PAUL'S COMMISSIONING

Paul's own letters only hint at the experience that transformed his whole worldview:

> But when God, who had set me apart before I was born and called me through his grace, was pleased to reveal his Son to me, so that I might proclaim him among the Gentiles, I did not confer with any human being, nor did I go up to Jerusalem to those who were apostles before me, but I went away at once into Arabia, and afterwards I returned to Damascus. (1:15–17)

Paul's language places his experience in line with a prophetic call. It has a formulaic similarity to the way the prophet Jeremiah described his religious experience: "Now the word of the LORD came to me, saying "Before I formed you in the womb I knew you, and before you were born I consecrated you; I appointed you a prophet to the nations" (Jer. 1:4–5). The designation "to be known or set apart before birth" expresses God's intimate knowledge of the person. The message given in the experience and to be announced is a divine word mediated through the prophet. Paul's self-designation at the beginning of Romans reinforces this sense of commission: "Paul, a servant of Jesus Christ, called to be an apostle, set apart for the gospel of God..." (Rom. 1:1). Like other prophets, Paul's experience of divine reality is wrapped in an experience of being called to do something.

Like Jeremiah, who was sent to "the nations," to Gentiles, Paul was called to go to those outside the people of Israel. His message would portray the inclusionary character of God's offer of salvation through Jesus. Like his fellow evangelists, Paul believed salvation was promised to those in the covenant.[3]

With them, Paul was convinced that the event of resurrection had begun the eschatological time. Thus their acute concern with membership. But in contrast to his opponents' soteriology, which correlated acceptance of the covenant with obeying the law, Paul correlated Gentile acceptance with the means of his own crossing over from one Judaism to another, religious conversion.

In the aftermath of Paul's experience of the risen Jesus came both continuity and change.[4] Before, he was a passionately religious Pharisee. Afterwards, he was a passionately religious messianic Jew. In this "crossing over," Paul had to undertake not only a reformulation of his religious views, as Larry Hurtado writes, but "indeed his whole religious 'self.'"[5] One of the most significant changes was Paul's view of Gentile conversion and inclusion into the people of God. Before his mystical Christ experience, he likely shared the belief of other Pharisees that Gentiles must become full proselytes to Judaism in order to share in Israel's biblical promises. His own conversion experience brought about a complete turn in his views. In light of God's raising the crucified Jesus, Paul became convinced that Gentiles were to share in these promises as *Gentiles* — not as the pagan Gentiles they had been but not living as Jews either. The "circle of those whom God accepts" was now defined by Paul as those who have faith in Jesus. No longer were the "identity markers" of a Jewish way of living the requirement for God's acceptance.[6]

Paul's experience of the risen Christ transformed the way he understood God's raising a crucified man from the dead. Instead of seeing "crucified man" and Messiah — God's anointed one — as a contradiction in terms, Paul saw an analogy between Jesus and the Gentiles.[7] According to Deut. 21:23, the one who "hangs on a tree" dies the death of a sinner (3:13), an outsider to the law. The ultimate outsiders, however, were not violators of the covenant but outsiders to it. At the heart of Paul's openness to Gentiles was his conviction that God's validation of the crucified outsider Jesus signaled God's validation of them. Gentiles, too, were offered the means to overcome their separation from the one true God proclaimed by Israel and known now through Jesus Christ.

Although Paul's experience happened several years after the death of Jesus, it gave him the essential criterion by which he could call himself an *apostle*. An apostle, like James or Mary Magdalene, was one who had "seen the risen Lord." In recounting Jesus' appearances, Paul puts himself in line with the apostles who knew Jesus: "Then he appeared to James, then to all the other disciples. Last of all, as to one untimely born, he appeared also to me" (1 Cor. 5:8). Paul's two questions to the Corinthians reinforce the connection: "Am I not an apostle? Have I not seen Jesus our Lord?" (1 Cor. 9:1).

That Paul underwent a profound religious experience is certain. As a "conversion," however, it was a reorientation within Judaism. Calvin Roetzel emphasizes that Paul "nowhere repudiated his native religion. And had he repudiated one expression of Judaism, would that mean he repudiated all Judaisms?"[8] Paul's mystical experience motivated a shift in loyalties, a "crossing over" from Pharisaic Judaism to the messianic-eschatological Judaism of the Jesus-followers. The two Judaisms shared the religious horizon of Jewish eschatological expectations and hopes.[9] For the Pharisaic Paul, these hopes were future, as yet unrealized. For the Christ-proclaimer Paul, the event of resurrection had initiated the time of their fulfillment. As Richard Horsley and Neil Silberman write, Paul's own "brilliant celestial vision of the Risen Jesus offered him a stunning apocalyptic vision. It confirmed that God had indeed begun to inaugurate a new age for Israel. . . . [It] brought about a far-reaching transformation in his life. . . . He looked forward to a new era of human existence, in which life on earth would be transformed."[10]

To speak, then, of Paul as a convert or apostate from Judaism is misleading. Paul's "language, his Scriptures, his holy symbols, and his institutions were and remained Jewish, and his personal reflections suggest a continuing attachment."[11] Christians have assumed not only that Paul no longer understood himself as a Jew but also that his ideas were so different from Judaism. But, as Daniel Boyarin argues, Paul lived and died "convinced that he was a Jew living out Judaism." He represents, "*one option which Judaism could take* in the first century."[12] The emergence of "Messianic Judaism" alongside Pharisaic Judaism and other groups represents "one option" that Judaism could take in the diverse tapestry of first-century Jewish life. Paul took his own role to be an extension of this diversity by announcing to Gentile women and men that, as believers, they, too, were members of Israel's covenant.

Jewish Pluralism in Paul's Time

The term *Second Temple Judaism* encompasses a period from the end of the Babylonian Exile to the destruction of Jerusalem and the Temple by the Romans (530 B.C.E.–70 C.E.). It comprises an ethnic people whose national identity was shaped by their religious faith and symbols.

Second Temple Judaism is better described as a way of life than a religion. Jewish life was made up of diverse, far-flung, and competing groups, including Sadducees, Pharisees, Hasideans, Essenes, Therapeutae, Jewish Hellenists, and Apocalyptics.[13] Says Gabriele Boccaccini:

We are now much more conscious that Judaism is to be seen not as an ideologically homogeneous unit but...as a set of different ideological systems in competition with one another....A plurality of groups, movements, and traditions of thought coexisted in a dialectical relationship, which was sometimes polemical but never disengaged. This complex and pluralistic period, however, has a clear, distinct, and unitary personality. The multiple and diverse answers offered by the different groups come from the same urgent questions.[14]

Tal Ilan describes Jewish society in the Second Temple period as "highly heterogenous." "Different groups lived by different versions of the law."[15] The Jewish movement proclaiming Jesus as messiah was situated within this heterogeneity and under Roman rule. Like other Judaisms, "Messianic Judaism" grounded its existence in the biblical promises and eschatological hopes found in the Torah and other Jewish writings. Paul came into it steeped in the Hebrew tradition. He was one of many Pharisees to join the movement.[16]

As a Jewish party, the Pharisees took to heart that God's mandate was living the way of the Torah. Living this distinctive lifestyle as a Jew is what is meant by "works of the law."[17] The Jewish historian Josephus refers to the Pharisees with admiration as a leading sect. While their name means "separated ones," they were not a separatist group, as were the Essenes. They originated as a lay group whose protest of political accommodation and corruption in elite Jewish circles took the form of an accentuated identification with the Torah. From the Torah they appropriated the priestly injunction to separate from other nations and sought to adapt to ordinary life the standards of purity designated for priests. They were devoted to applying the law of the temple cult to everyday life.[18] It was this that set them apart from others.

Pharisees were concerned first and foremost with Jewish identity. Roman occupation was an ever-present threat to the continued existence of the Jews as a distinctive people. The Pharisees responded by emphasizing Israel's identity or boundary markers.[19] Ritual practices such as circumcision, following food laws, and observing the Sabbath took on highly symbolic meaning. They considered observances of these practices test cases for covenant loyalty.

The status of the Pharisees as an opposition party attracted the support of wealthy women. In fact, their one time in political power was granted to them by a woman. "It is a well-known historical fact," Tal Ilan writes, "that only during the nine short years of Queen Shelamzion's rule did the Pharisees gain the upper hand in Palestinian politics and were in a position to dictate their ideas of how to govern the Jewish people."[20] The queen favored the Pharisees, as did many women, but not because their views of women were favorable.[21] Their attitude was hostile in fact. Their eventual heirs, the rabbis of the second century C.E., were even more hostile to women. The collection of their reflections, the Mishnah, "was edited in such a way as to curtail, diminish and censor women's rights and participation in Jewish life both in general and in detail."[22]

Pharisaic Judaism required of interested Gentiles obedience to the written and oral Torah as taught and practiced by the rabbis. The process of Gentile conversion entailed thorough instruction, a change of lifestyle, circumcision for men, immersion and sacrifice for all, followed by a strict and permanent regimen of attention to purity and dietary prohibitions.[23] Converted Gentiles, now belonging to the covenant people, became Jewish men and women.

PAUL'S ZEALOUS FAITH

Paul's religious worldview was shaped by his familial identification with Pharisaic Judaism in the Hellenistic Diaspora and
by his own studies as a Pharisee.[24] Acts 22:3 portrays Paul as
a student in Jerusalem with Gamaliel, a leading Pharisee. This
biographical detail may have more to do with the writer of Acts
wanting to identify Paul with the liberal wing of the Pharisaic
party, with which Gamaliel is associated, than with Paul's actual
history. Gamaliel is portrayed as arguing before the Sanhedrin
for toleration of Jews who were proclaiming the risen Jesus as
Savior (Acts 5:33–39).

Paul described himself as a persecutor of these believers (Gal.
1:13; 1 Cor. 15:9). He put his opposition to the Jesus-followers
in the context of being "zealous for the traditions of my an-
cestors" (1:14). The word *zēlotēs*, zealous, may mean that he
interpreted the obligation of Jews to do "works of the law" in
a conservative fashion. Or it may refer to his dedication to the
identity of the people of Israel and fear that the Jesus-followers
posed a threat in some way. Beverly Gaventa finds the word
revealing of Paul's self-understanding prior to his conversion. It:

> frequently appears in the Jewish literature of the Hellenis-
> tic period in connection with zeal for the law of God,
> which may require suffering, and zeal that results in pun-
> ishment of those who disobey the law. Moreover, *zēlotēs*
> as zeal for the law and against the disobedient is promi-
> nent in 1 and 2 Maccabees.... Thus, Paul's use of *zēlotēs*
> connects him with the zealous Jews of the Maccabean pe-
> riod. He saw himself as following in the tradition of those
> who acted forcefully to defend that which was proper to
> Judaism.[25]

In the Acts of the Apostles, Luke portrays Paul's opposition to Jewish women and men who were disciples of the crucified Jesus and members of the "Way" (Acts 9:2) more graphically than Paul does himself. Paul belongs to the "strictest sect of our religion" (Acts 26:5).[26] He breathes "threats and murder against the disciples of the Lord" (Acts 9:1). He watches and approves of an angry mob's stoning of Stephen, one of the first of the Jesus disciples to preach publicly (Acts 7:54–8:1). He "locked up many" in prison, tried to "force them to blaspheme," was "furiously enraged" at them, and "pursued them even to foreign cities" (Acts 26:9–11).

What was Paul offended by? Two issues were likely factors. One may have been the scandalous contradiction between Jesus' crucifixion, the death of a criminal, and the proclamation of him as Messiah. The second issue may have been either the food shared or the unrestricted social interaction of Jews with Gentiles when Jesus-followers met in their religious gatherings. For a Jew, and especially for a Pharisee, purity required the separation of Jew from Gentile. If this mingling gave offense, it was because Paul considered Gentiles impure and eating with them a covenant violation. If his attention was on the food, it was likely the suspicion that Gentile food (especially meat) was associated with pagan temple sacrifice.[27] These matters within Judaism were important and volatile. Paul was deeply involved with them, and his radical shift in loyalties was therefore all the more remarkable.

Any one of these reasons could have been the cause for offense to one on the theologically conservative end of the Jewish spectrum. But it may also have been that Paul feared that an outspoken Jewish messianic group would incite the violence of the imperial order against Jews. This fear would not have been unrealistic. In 49 C.E. the edict of the emperor Claudius expelled all Jews from Rome due to disturbances blamed on Christians. They were allowed to return only after Nero eliminated the ban in 54 C.E.[28]

The Jesus-followers divided into three groups on the place of the law. Alan Segal describes all three positions as growing out of Pharisaism.[29] The brother of Jesus and leader of the Jerusalem church, James, believed that the entire Jewish law remained in effect. Peter's position was more moderate. Paul's eventual position was not strictly Pharisaic but developed out of his rejection of it. It was not a complete departure from Pharisaic Judaism when Paul maintained that Gentiles did not need to become Jews to share in the world to come, for this was a position Pharisees debated and some accepted as well. But in insisting that the boundaries between Jewish and Gentile communities be dissolved, Paul overstepped what Pharisaic Judaism could accommodate.

It was not just James but many of Jesus' first Jewish followers who believed that their affirmation of Jesus as God's Messiah did not in any way signify that living as a Jew should end. Acts 21:20 describes "thousands of believers" among the Jews who were "zealous for the law." The later authority given the Pauline letters in the tradition overshadows the historical reality that James's position on the law was the majority one and Paul's the minority one. Noting Luke's treatment of James in Acts, John Painter writes that Luke "sought to minimize the role of James because he was aware that James represented a hard-line position on the place of circumcision and the keeping of the law, a position that Luke himself did not wish to retain."[30]

Heikki Räisänen speculates that the Galatian situation may have been due to the growing number of Pharisees whose views reflected a "thoroughly Biblical position" joining the movement.

They believed that circumcision, the sign of God's covenant, and obedience to Torah prescriptions had to be taken seriously, even in the eschatological situation.[31] In Joseph Fitzmyer's judgment, Paul's opponents were from Palestine and theologically even more conservative than James.[32] Their position that Gentiles must come into Israel in the normal way, even in the eschatological time, reflects an underlying conviction that salvation is reserved to those who adhere to the covenant and live as the law mandates. Their claim that Paul was not preaching the true gospel (1:7) is a criticism that he did not require Torah-observance of Gentile women and men. It is easy to mistake their concern. Obedience to the law is not an end in itself but a means. For these evangelists, Paul had put the Gentiles believers' salvation at risk by not having them live as the God of Israel had commanded Israel to live.

Paul's position was clear: salvation and Gentile membership in the people of God is no longer contingent upon the appropriation of the national identity of Jews or religious identity markers.[33] Further, in the Diaspora assemblies, "equality of access to salvation" applied now to women. For Paul's challengers, fidelity to God required obedience to the law and the law restricts women from the same participation in the religious cult as a man. Were they offended by the presumption of equality of women with men in these assemblies? With themselves?

Paul's Symbolic Horizon

Paul interpreted his experience of the risen Jesus through the symbols of Israel's self-identity. His mission to Gentile women and men presupposed and utilized them. In the end, he was instrumental in transforming them.

At the core of Israel's self-understanding was the symbol of election. The biblical writers emphasize that Israel had been chosen to be a special people. Ultimately, Israel's task was to draw "all nations" to the one true God. Paul's mission as "apostle to the Gentiles" fits within this image of Israel's election. As noted, his interpretation of Gentile inclusion is not unheard of in Jewish thinking in the first century, though it is not the mainstream position. It elicited criticism and opposition even from within the Jesus movement. As taken up by the early patristic writers, and employed for their own ends, Paul's view will threaten the meaning of election for Israel.

The land of Israel was the second symbol of Israel's self-identity. The biblical writer portrays the land as God's promise in a covenant made with Abraham (Gen. 15:7, 18; 17:8). A third symbol, covenant, constituted Israel's understanding of the human and divine relationship. The original meaning of covenant was political. As a stronger king enters into a contractual relationship with a weaker king, the biblical writers depict Yahweh's entering into a relationship of fidelity with humankind, first with Noah (Gen. 6:18), then with Abraham (Gen. 17:10), and, after the Exodus, with Moses at Sinai (Exod. 19:1).

Here, as in the political arena, there were promises and obligations on both sides. Yahweh's promise was a self-gift, "to be your God..." (Deut. 26: 17). Israel's obligation was "to keep God's covenant" (Exod. 19:5), meaning to do God's will. In the perspective of the priestly writer, Israel was to be "a kingdom of priests and a holy people."[34]

To Abraham was given the sign of covenant membership and the command for it: "This is my covenant, which you shall keep, between me and you and your offspring after you: Every male among you shall be circumcised....Any uncircumcised male who is not circumcised in the flesh of his foreskin shall be cut off from his people; he has broken my covenant" (Gen. 17:10, 14). Embedded in this story is a foretelling of Hebrew slavery in Egypt and the promise that they will return to the land (Gen. 15:14). Their journey back to Canaan is marked by the giving of the law to Moses (Ex. 20).

The texts of Abraham, the sign of the covenant, and Moses' receiving the law as the means by which Israel was to live were foundational for Israelite and later Jewish identity. In responding to his challengers in Galatia, Paul has to relativize their unequivocal character and find another place from which to make his own counter-case and to back it with the authority of scripture.

Paul found that place in Abraham's believing or trust in God (3:6). He created an analogy with which to legitimate the inclusion of Gentiles in Israel. "Just as Abraham 'believed God, and it was reckoned to him as righteousness,' so, you see, those who believe are descendants of Abraham" (3:6–7). He assured the women and men who had responded to his preaching that "those who believe are blessed with Abraham who believed" (3:9). To them, once outsiders to Israel's salvation, the blessing of Abraham has come to them through the crucified Christ (3:14).[35]

As we have seen, Paul's judgment, grounded in his own conversion, that Gentile women and men were to share in Israel's covenant without becoming Jews was not shared uniformly by other Jews, even other Jesus-followers.[36] Given Paul's various trials and tribulations — being thrown out of synagogues, whipped, and jailed — it is apparent that his position was offensive to some and a hopeless contradiction to others. The main difficulty was severing righteousness from Torah-observance, a split that would have been inconceivable to most Jews.[37] Moses' speech suggests why:

See, I am setting before you today a blessing and a curse:
the blessing, if you obey the commandments of the LORD
your God that I am commanding you today; and the curse,
if you do not obey the commandments of the LORD your
God, but turn from the way that I am commanding you today, to follow other gods that you have not known. (Deut.
11:26–28)

The symbol of the Torah thus unified all others. The theologies of election and covenant shape its dominant perspective.
As God's gift to Israel, the Torah provides the means for obedience to God. It is the way of holiness. The Deuteronomistic
writer is clear about the absolute character of Israel's covenant
obligation: "You must follow exactly the path that the LORD
your God has commanded you, so that you may live, and that
it may go well with you, and that you may live long in the land
that you are to possess" (Deut. 5:32–33).

For some Jews, "the Torah was both a divine law and also,
for those living in Judaea, the law of the land, its earthly constitution."[38] Its mandates created a way of living that set Jews
apart from non-Jews outside the people of Israel, and within
Israel, male from female. Inside and outside the covenant were
distinguished as sacred and profane realms. The holiness laws
were the means by which Israel was to meet its overarching
command: "You are to be a people holy to the LORD your God"
(Deut. 26:19). The Torah gave mandates to Jewish men and
women for social, economic, political, religious, and gender interactions, the norm for righteousness, and expression of their
hopes as a people singled out by God to be God's own.

But even among insiders this did not mean "that all Jewish practice and belief in the law was uniform."[39] What Jews
brought to the Torah was a broad range of interpretation

and application. Paul believed that Christ's death removed the boundary of the covenant between insider and outsider. While he did not reject the validity of the law for Jews, his soteriological exclusivism made it difficult to maintain. His foundational premise was that Christ died to save Jews and Gentiles. Jews must enter into the new assembly to be saved. But to be part of a community that included unrestricted interaction with Gentiles would put Torah-observant Jews in covenant violation.[40] In fact, Paul's Christocentric view of redemption allowed no other means of salvation.

Paul's religious horizon thus continued to be complexly shaped by these symbols after his revelatory experience. He appealed to one of the primary figures in Israel's tradition. All those who believe are "descendants of Abraham" (3:7), "Abraham's offspring, heirs according to the promise" (3:29). He paraphrases Deuteronomy, "Cursed is everyone who hangs on a tree" (3:13; Deut. 21:22). Jesus is the "Christ," the anointed one, Messiah, for whom Jews await (1:1). Paul wishes peace on the "Israel of God" (6:16). Larry Hurtado emphasizes the ongoing centrality of these symbols for Paul:

> Though he certainly redefines what is required for Gentiles to be included in the benefits of the promise (faith in Christ rather than Torah observance), it is clear that the very Jewish categories of Abrahamic promise, covenant, the purposes of God giving the Torah, and other matters as well, all continue to be of vital meaning and importance to Paul.[41]

Referring to the messianic communities in the land of Israel, especially the Jerusalem church, Ekkehard and Wolfgang Stegemann write that, "There is no reason to doubt the ongoing Jewish identity of the followers of Jesus and their loyalty to the institutions and basic convictions of Israel."[42] About Paul personally, Calvin Roetzel emphasizes, "Certainly there were tensions between Paul and his Jewish peers, but those were tensions that inevitably came from being a liminal or marginal figure. They were intra-mural, not extra-mural. In sum, Paul was born a Jew, lived as a Jew, and in all likelihood died as a Jew."[43] The dispute in Galatia over Gentile converts, in James Dunn's words, is "entirely in Jewish terms," set within the framework of election, covenant, and Torah.[44]

Jewish Restoration Eschatology

A further Jewish horizontal element for Paul was eschatological expectation. The longstanding reality of foreign domination created fertile ground for the eschatological hopes of Jews in the first century. Israel's eschatological expectations and symbols arise out of the experience of evil. They express the hope that one day God will act against evil and that God's reign would replace the reign of evil. That will be the decisive time. Meaning "end-time," the *eschaton* is within history, not the end of history.

The biblical image of the "reign of evil" captures the sense of its pervasiveness. Evil distorts the created order, not simply in terms of individual morality but also in terms of social relations, structures, and institutions. What should be (good) is not, and what should not be (evil) is. What dominates present history is evil — injustice, inequality, violence, oppression. In particular, the evil that threatens Israel in the first century is Rome.

The evil giving rise to eschatological hopes is concrete, not abstract. It is political occupation and oppression by foreign powers, the reality of foreign rulers, standing armies, crushing taxation, loss of ancestral lands and collaboration of the native elite with the oppressor. No longer an independent people, Israel's distinctiveness was threatened by the imposition of or willing assimilation to Greco-Roman customs and norms.

The proper responses to foreign domination, the danger of assimilation, and the threat to Jewish identity were matters of intense disagreement among Jews within Palestine and the Diaspora. In particular, the issue of endangered Jewish identity is in the background of the dispute in Galatia over Gentile converts.

What was a common element in the religious worldview of Jews was the conviction that the reign of evil has distorted creation. Jewish hopes for the future are hopes that God will restore creation to the way it should be. God will punish evil-doers and vindicate the righteous. Three symbols are important in this restoration eschatology: *resurrection, messiah*, and the *basileia tou theou*.

The event of resurrection is a three-fold signal for the beginning of the eschatological age, the impending divine judgment, and, given the window between the two, a time for repentance.

In ancient Israel the term *Messiah* refers to God's "anointed one." The ritual of anointing with oil accompanied the consecration of a priest or king. Transcendent to the historical realm, divine reality acts in history through mediators, and the Messiah is God's agent.

The Greek term *basileia* is translated by various English terms, including *reign, rule, kingdom of God.* Translating *basileia* as *empire* communicates the way in which this symbol functioned as a contrast of empires and as a means of social critique. The announcement and vision of God's *basileia* was central to Jesus' preaching. Two empires, two sets of values vie. One empire is characterized by compassion for the marginalized, the other by its creation of the marginalized. One empire is characterized by inclusion of all at the table, the other by exclusion of all but a few from the resources for sustaining life and well-being. The inclusiveness of the Pauline communities embodied the redemptive experience of God's *basileia*.

NEW CREATION

For Jews, the Torah marked the social boundary between the spheres of holy and unholy or, to put it in terms of purity, between pure and impure.[45] Holiness and purity were contingent on following the way of the Torah. In a similar fashion, "being in Christ" (3:28; 5:5) was Paul's creation of a social boundary for Gentiles as God's people.[46] The women and men who belong to this new community "define a new social reality, different from the reality of both Jews and Jewish Christians."[47] Paul's principle for membership and salvation was the same for women and men. Their initiation through baptism was gender-neutral, too.

Through Christ, distinctions among human beings that mark some as persons and others as non-persons have been eliminated (3:28). Religious, class, and gender distinctions meant everything in the ancient world, but the baptismal confession in 3:28 suggests they have no longer have bearing on salvation or before God.[48] The assembly restores the original equality of women and men given in Genesis 1:27.[49]

Paul appropriates the familiar language of covenant to designate the new Gentile assemblies of women and men believers as the "new covenant" (1 Cor. 11:25; 2 Cor. 3:6).[50] While he uses terms, like this, that had become part of the Jesus tradition, he also uses different ones. The new social reality of the *ekklēsia* is a "new creation" (6:15). What Christ has done was not contrasted with Moses but with Adam. Just as Adam's sin determined the fate of the world, so too would Christ's death.

Further, the received covenantal language cannot accommodate what Sanders calls Paul's "participationist transfer terms," such as the believer's dying with Christ and to the power of sin. At the core of Paul's theology was not the ratification of a new covenant but receiving new life.

For Paul, that Gentile women and men received the Spirit in baptism confirmed that God's inclusion of them in the eschatological covenant was to be based on their religious conversion, not on their becoming Jewish proselytes and themselves appropriating the lifestyle of Jews.[51] The expectation of the Spirit runs deep in Jewish restoration eschatology.[52] The giving of the Spirit would signify the revitalization of Israel. But it was expected that the Spirit would be given to Jews and only in the context of law-observance, not to non-proselyte Gentiles. Within this context Paul interpreted the reception of the Spirit by Gentile women and men as the fulfillment of the promise (3:14), the inauguration of the fullness of time (4:4–6), and evidence that the recipients were sons and daughters of God. Elisabeth Schüssler Fiorenza writes that "In the new Spirit-filled community of equals all distinctions of race, religion, class and gender are abolished. All are equal and one in Christ Jesus."[53] For women, Spirit-filled prophecy and possession of wisdom meant an enhanced social status that they could not otherwise enjoy.[54] Distinguishing the Diaspora communities from Palestinian, James Dunn identifies their central feature: "The Pauline concept of church and ministry *differs from the pattern that evolved at Jerusalem* in that it was essentially a concept of charismatic authority. . . ."[55]

Just as the Jerusalem Temple was holy because of God's dwelling in it, so now the "assembly is the temple, and since the temple is holy, the assembly is holy."[56] The divine presence was now experienced in the indwelling of God as Spirit. Calvin

Roetzel notes that like the Qumran community Paul used the temple metaphor in a self-referential way, but his use of it as an egalitarian metaphor was distinctive: "He made the plural 'you all' refer to all his addressees as holy rather than to a priestly, conventicle community as was the case among the priests at Qumran *and* Jerusalem."[57] In part Jewish life was ordered by the Temple and its rituals, but in a far more extensive way purity laws mapped out human living. The law functions as a purity boundary. A purity system renders some human beings nonpersons by virtue of bodily defect, sickness, or despised profession. Purity is linked with ethnicity (Jews *versus* non-Jews), class (masters *versus* slaves), and gender (males *versus* females). The impurity of women — due to blood and lactation associated with menstruation and childbirth — restricts their participation in the social and religious spheres.[58]

Of significance in Paul's appropriation of the temple metaphor for the Gentile assemblies is the fact that he makes no appeal to purity laws or to any other cultural or religious norm that would assign women a lower status and exclude them from full participation in the religious cult. Without purity as a category, persons in the assembly are not differentiated by gender in this way. Neither is holiness correlated with purity. Accordingly, there is no basis for exemptions — which translate into exclusions — for women. Rights, duties, and obligations are not designated by gender. In a world structured by purity, the "egalitarian" use of the temple metaphor to designate women as holy would have been striking.[59]

We will look next at how Paul's complex religious worldview, profoundly formed and reformed by his experience of Christ, interacted with the particular features of Diaspora Judaism as they developed and were disputed in the Christ-communities of Galatia.

Chapter Three

CHALLENGES AND CHALLENGERS IN GALATIA

P AUL MOUNTS AN INTENSE COUNTER in Galatians to the challenge of fellow evangelists competing with him for the hearts and minds of Gentile women and men he had converted to Christ. He stood in immediate danger of losing those whose religious conversion his preaching had prompted and with whom he had created charismatic religious assemblies. Kept by distance from intervening in person, Paul has only the power of rhetoric to defend the kind of assemblies he depicts as the "new creation" (6:15). His sweeping dismissal of the law for Gentiles gives no hint of the compelling power of the argument of the law against him. Drawing his authority straight from God, he so effectively undercuts the evangelists who disagreed with him that few Christians have suspected that his opponents, not Paul, held the more authoritative position on the salvation of Gentiles. Paul's fear of their potential success is palpable. He rebukes those suspected of betrayal, inveighs against potential defectors, curses his opponents, and wishes castration on those who choose circumcision. The "truth of the gospel" (2:5) is characterized as performative: "You were running well," he says. "Who prevented you from obeying the truth?" (5:7).[1]

THE GALATIAN ASSEMBLIES

Where did Paul send this letter? To whom? Uncharacteristically, Paul did not address the letter's recipients by their city. Exactly where these women and men were located remains an open question. The designation *Galatia* can refer to an ethnic group as well as a region. The fact that the Romans changed the boundaries of the region complicates the geographical question even more.[2]

The groups to whom Paul writes were likely exclusively Gentile.[3] Paul offers little hint of any presence of Jewish Christ-believers. He does not allude to men who are already circumcised, for example, alongside those who are contemplating accepting the sign (5:1). The participants in these assemblies seem to fit under this one address of those whose religious origins were pagan: "Formerly, when you did not know God, you were enslaved to beings that by nature are not gods" (4:8).

Paul had drawn Gentile women and men together into a religious assembly by his preaching "freedom in Christ" (5:1). Their understanding of "freedom" was not abstract, as Hans Dieter Betz emphasizes:

> For them "freedom" was not merely a theological notion, but they regarded themselves as free from "this evil world" with its repressive social, religious, and cultural laws and conventions. They had left behind the cultural and social distinctions between Greeks and non-Greeks, the religious distinctions between Jews and non-Jews, the social systems of slavery and the subordination of women.[4]

Paul founded what is described by modern anthropologists as "fictive kinship groups."[5] Like Jesus and others who left their families and villages to hear John or like Jesus' disciples when they followed him, these Gentile women and men have symbolically stepped "outside the kinship network" in which they were born and raised.[6] Paul creates the group as a new or alternative family by his use of familial terms. They are members of "God's family," (1:2), "brothers and sisters" (3:15), "children of God" (1:11; 3:26).[7] While Paul laid claim to the authority embedded in his revelatory experience and commission as an apostle (1:15–17), he called them "friends" (4:12). He sends his letter to the "churches of Galatia" (1:2), to several groups, not one. Their familiarity with one another or location in relation to one another is uncertain.

In the first-century context of Paul, "assembly" gives a better sense of the Greek *ekklēsia* and its meaning of "gathered together" or "called out" than does "church." To the modern reader, "church" evokes the image of a building or an institutional structure. It generates an anachronistic image, in its original secular context of the Athenian democracy, *ekklēsia* referred to the calling together of all citizens to vote. "All citizens" did not actually denote "all people" but elite males.[8] All believers were citizens in the Jesus community, the *ekklēsia tou theou*, however.[9] Women and men gathered in the name of Christ (1 Thess. 2:14). The baptismal confession in Gal. 3:28 grounds the defining feature of the assembly and of redemption, namely, the absence of privilege and difference, which structure hierarchical relations and systematize domination.

Jewish Missionaries and Gentile Proselytes

By the time of Paul, Jews outside the land of Israel had engaged in successful proselytism of Gentiles for centuries. By coming into contact with other missionary philosophies, such as Epicureanism, Stoicism, and Cynicism, Diaspora Jews were under pressure to defend their own beliefs. Missionary work provided a context for such a defense. "Judaism, if it could present itself as a superior ethical code, a systematic philosophy predating the Greeks, or the greatest mystery cult, might win adherents."[10]

Evidence of Jewish proselytizing activity is also given in the prohibitions of it. "The success of Jewish proselytism," as Wayne Meeks points out, "is indicated by the Roman laws and police measures which were taken from time to time to inhibit it, beginning with the expulsion of Jews from Rome by Cornelius Hispalus in 139 B.C., reported by Valerius Maximus."[11]

Widespread and successful proselytism is also considered a factor in the dramatic Jewish population increase in the Hellenistic period.[12] The Diaspora was a congenial environment for Gentile conversion, "first of all because there were greater numbers of potential converts living side by side with Jews, engaging in commercial and cultural contact with them and fighting alongside them."[13] Proselytizers were especially successful among women, many of whom became "God-fearers" or sympathizers, if not full proselytes. The heightening of Jewish messianic hopes from the second century B.C.E. was accompanied by a heightened Gentile interest in Judaism. While Paul brought a new savior, the Diaspora was already fertile ground for his preaching.

Economic factors came into play for both the Jewish proselytizer and the Gentile proselyte. Economic and political alliances Jews undertook with Gentiles facilitated trade. Such was the case with King Izates in Adiabene in Mesopotamia early in the first century C.E. For Gentiles, conversion opened international sources of capital. Once they became Jewish, merchants could borrow money without interest. It was beneficial to be part of a group in which economic cooperation was facilitated by a Jewish presence in influential commercial positions in cities around the Mediterranean world and beyond. But philosophical and economic factors did not exhaust Jewish motivation for proselytism. The Alexandrian Jewish philosopher Philo spoke of the conversion of non-Jews as a moral matter. In his view, the only way for Gentiles to live "a sound and steadfast life" was through Judaism. Philo's moral concern was grounded in the dominant theology of covenant. Membership in the covenant was salvation. "In Judaism," Alan Segal writes, "the urge to proselytize never abated until the Christian emperors made conversion to Judaism a crime."[14]

Palestinian and Diaspora Judaisms differed in their expectations and requirements for Gentile conversion. In the land of Israel expectations were fairly uniform: Gentiles should do what Israel was expected to do. For a Palestinian Jew, James Dunn writes, "it would be virtually impossible to conceive of participation in God's covenant, and so in God's covenant righteousness, apart from these observances, these works of the law."[15]

In Diaspora Judaism, by contrast, proselytizing was characterized by a broader range of views. Most like Palestinian Jews, Shammaite Pharisees thought Gentile conversion required full appropriation of Jewish identity through Torah-observance. At the other end of the spectrum, Jewish Hellenists accepted God-fearers — men and women just shy of full conversion — without complete Torah-observance.[16] As a Christ-follower, Paul shared the view found among Greek-speaking Hellenistic Jews that God-fearing Gentiles were the complete equals of Jews.[17]

Whether Paul engaged in proselytizing as a Pharisee before his conversion experience is unclear. Paul's question, "Why am I still being persecuted if *I am still preaching circumcision?*" suggests evangelizing activity (5:11).[18] Some argue that Paul's references to his zeal for the law or being zealous for the law evoke the perspective of Shammaite Pharisees and their strict interpretation of Gentile conversion.[19]

Jews had different views about the status of converts, too. For Philo, proselytes received the privileges of native-born Jews.[20] In the rabbinic literature, the status of the proselyte is described as that of a newborn babe, born now as one of the people of God. Not everyone thought so favorably about Gentile converts, however. The Essenes are one example. Known through the discovery of manuscripts near the Dead Sea, they excluded proselytes. In fact, their exclusionary theology went beyond the standard distinction between covenant insiders and outsiders. The Essenes believed that only members of their community were destined for salvation.[21]

Gentile Converts

Gentile conversion seems to be a post-exilic phenomenon.[22] Because in the pre-exilic period the people, land, and God of Israel had been indissolubly bound together, the practice of conversion was absent. After the Babylonian Exile and loss of political independence, however, Israelites became "Jews." That is, the foundational texts, practices, and lines of Second-Temple Judaisms emerge, and a Gentile could convert to Judaism and become a Jew.

Judaism attracted Gentiles for a variety of reasons — its monotheism, antiquity, moral life, and the social cohesion of its community.[23] Says Louis Feldman, "Many undoubtedly were attracted, in a period of general political, economic, and social instability to a community which, by regulating itself, had found inner security. The fellowship which came through eating together, attending weekly meetings, and avoiding the same foods may have enticed the lonely."[24] Jewish compassion was also a catalyst for conversion, he says. "Poor Gentiles, once converted, could benefit from the extraordinarily effective charities of the Jews."[25]

Philo of Alexandria distinguished three aspects of the conversion — religious, ethical, and social — of Gentiles to Judaism.[26] Central is the convert's change in worship from the many gods of paganism to the one true God of Israel. This reorientation is one of turning to the truth within the context of the Jewish law. With the reorientation to truth comes a similar reorientation to genuine value, from the values exhibited in a pagan way of life to those exhibited in the virtuous way of life of Jews. The third aspect of Gentile conversion is social. Jewish proselytes leave their "family, their country, their customs. Abraham is the prototype of the proselyte who leaves his home in this way (*Virt.* 214)...proselytes have entered the Jewish nation...."[27] Paul picks up on this image of Abraham in his conflict with fellow evangelists in the Galatian context.

Jewish practices and festivals remained attractive to Gentiles after the first century, with Gentile Christians "crossing over into Judaism, at least in certain practices and customs"[28] Noting Ignatius of Antioch in the second century C.E. and Chrysostom and Aphrahat in the fourth century C.E., Lee Martin McDonald writes that "The church fathers frequently warned Christians against being attracted to Judaism and identifying with the Jews, who, they claimed, were blind, stubborn, and had killed Christ."[29] The hostility with which the early church fathers responded to this situation is a clue that this "crossing over" was no small or occasional problem but a genuine and perennial concern. Agobard, archbishop of Lyons, warned Christians in the ninth century C.E. against being led astray and chastised those who had been. McDonald writes that:

It is hard to believe that all of these conversions to Judaism, or even Christian participation in Jewish festivals and other religious activities, could have taken place without significant missionary activity on the part of the Jews. Jewish proselytizing appears to have played a major role in producing some of the church's strongest invective against the Jews well into the Middle Ages.[30]

Gentile women and men pursued their attraction to Judaism in different degrees. These degrees were given names: *sympathizers* (attracted), *God-fearers* (attracted, took on some Jewish practices), *proselytes* (attracted, converted fully, became Jewish men and women, accepted Jewish covenant obligations).[31]

Conversion to Judaism was no small matter. It first required appropriation of Israel's covenant obligation: observing the Torah commands proper to women and those proper to men. By doing so, the converted Gentile became a member of the people of Israel.[32] Entrance into Israel — even if no longer an independent nation — required a denial of ancestral gods, native land, and family. "Philo and Josephus explicitly describe conversion to Judaism as the acquisition of a new citizenship (*politeia*) and contrast the openness of the Jewish citizenship with the restrictiveness of others."[33]

Fear of circumcision, then, was not the only factor that kept adult Gentile men at the status of "almost fully converted," or God-fearers. They remained bound to the civic duty to worship local deities, an obligation from which native-born Jews were exempt but converts to Judaism were not. They could be charged with "atheism" if they failed to worship as required.[34] So, says Louis Feldman, "To be a Jew created an immediate conflict in patriotism, inasmuch as religion in antiquity was regularly part of the state, and the Jew, ipso facto, could not worship the state's gods."[35]

The precariousness of social identity caused by conversion, especially for men, was significant. By their converting to Judaism, men forfeited their former identity. But their new identity within Judaism was not without ambiguity, writes Shaye Cohen:

> In the eyes of outsiders a proselyte "became" and could be called a Jew...but in the eyes of the Jews did the proselytes "become" Jews? Apparently not.... The rabbis state that when the conversion ceremony is complete the proselyte is "like an Israelite in all respects." But none of these passages demonstrates that the proselyte achieved real equality with the native born. The proselyte probably had an ambiguous status in the Jewish community.[36]

The issue of social identity may have been especially acute for men drawn to the Pauline assemblies. They had left pagan gods of the civic religion for the God of Israel, yet, lacking circumcision, they had not become Jewish either. Relations with both family and Jewish synagogue would have been strained.

What other rituals signaled the entrance of male converts to their new status, aside from circumcision? That remains an open question. In H. H. Rowley's judgment, evidence points to the Jewish practice prior to the Common Era of baptizing proselytes, although its origins are impossible to date.[37] Immersion was a powerful symbol in ancient Israel, as Richard A. Horsley and Neil Asher Silberman point out, not only for the removal of physical impurity but also as a metaphor for moral purification.[38] In Isaiah 1:16–17, Yahweh commands it: " 'Wash yourselves; make yourselves clean; remove the evil of your doings from my eyes; cease to do evil; learn to do good; seek justice, correct oppression; defend the fatherless, plead for the widow.'" In the Qumran scrolls, ritual immersion "signified that a profound change in character and social commitment had *already* been made."[39] Embedded in the performance of the ritual was a trenchant social critique. Declaration of community membership, "solemnly symbolized by the repeated ritual of baptism, meant that the bather had rejected the entire complex of economics, political institutions, and cultural expression that was being carried on in mainstream society."[40]

The Talmud, while it post-dates the first century, gives "trustworthy" evidence of the requirement for male proselytes to undergo both circumcision and baptism, and then to offer a sacrifice.[41] The ceremony for a woman proselyte was administered by men; but the proselyte was accompanied to the place of immersion by women, while the men stayed out of sight. Through the baptismal rite, the Gentile convert became a member of the covenant people and heir of the biblical promises. As a sincere believer in the faith of Judaism, the convert was admitted into the elect and its channel of grace.[42] Religious conversion was a rebirth and entrance to a wholly new life.

Immersion was a key symbol for John the Baptizer, too. In his apocalyptic preaching of the coming day of judgment, John made immersion available to all who would accept it.[43] The practice of immersion, with the ideas that accompanied it, also became the validating ritual of entry into the Pauline assemblies. "Paul defined one of the basic rites of conversion in Judaism, ritual immersion or baptism, as the prototypical rite of entrance to the new community as well."[44] Unlike circumcision, which applies only to male converts, baptism is gender-neutral. Women and men underwent the same ritual. This indifference to gender promoted the social integration of women into the community.[45] As in the other forms of Judaism, admission to the eschatological community was conceived as a channel of grace. But now the gift of God's own Spirit was understood to be received through membership (3:2).

Paul's Polemics

Against this background of Jewish missionary activity and Gentile conversion, Galatians provides an important polemical window into the pluralism that characterized the Jesus movement. But this window is problematic inasmuch as our sources reflect Paul's concerted effort to devalue the position and persons of his challengers in the minds of the Galatian women and men. They in turn were caught between Paul's interpretation of the *ekklēsia* of Gentile inclusion and the interpretation of the other evangelists. Paul's authority and conception of the social reality of the assembly were under acute threat, and his letter is not disinterested.

Whatever is to be said about Paul's theological position on Gentile women and men proselytes, in Galatians it is embedded in polemical language. Examples of language that accuses and attacks are not hard to find in the Hebrew tradition. The psalmists frequently rail against the wicked, the greedy, and oppressors, concluding at one point with the judgment about humanity that, "They have all gone astray, they are all perverse; there is no one who does good, no, not one" (Ps 14:2–3). In the prophetic Book of Amos, God throws out threats and curses, ridiculing the wealthy and dismissing the powerful. With particular vehemence, God rejects the ceremonies of public religion: "I hate, I despise your festivals, and take no delight in your solemn assemblies" (Amos 5:21). Through this invective, Amos separates himself from Jewish groups, in particular, the elite and representatives of "politically embedded religion" in the ancient world.[46]

Separation is the function of polemical language. "Rhetorically potent language," Scot McKnight writes, "is used throughout the ancient world to erect, fortify, and maintain the boundaries that distinguish one religious community from another or to separate, within the same religious community, the obedient from the disobedient."[47]

Paul's polemic separates the two missionary wings into one (his own) that is obedient to an agreement made in Jerusalem with James and others that Paul would go to the "uncircumcised," and another group (theirs) that is disobedient to the same agreement that they would go to the "circumcised" (2:7). Paul's unspoken but clear accusation is that these evangelists, by preaching against him in the Galatian assemblies, have violated the "right hand of fellowship" sealing this accord (2:9). Recalling the Jerusalem meeting serves a twofold purpose. It first exposes the other evangelists as dishonorable because of their breech of the agreement (2:1–10). But it also reinforces that the agreement included what he was going to tell these Gentiles and exactly what was understood as necessary for their inclusion in Israel's covenant of salvation (2:5, 14, 16–17).[48]

For centuries, Christians took Paul's polemical words for "the way it was." With Paul as the authoritative lens into the historical situation, readers took for granted that the other evangelists were interlopers and wrong to have come into assemblies Paul had founded. Paul's description of those "who are confusing you and want to pervert the gospel of Christ" (1:7) allowed subsequent Christians to conclude that the motives of these men were suspect and sinister. Even today, a more "sensitive

reading" of the motives and theology of the visiting evangelists raises questions about whether it does not take something
important away from Paul.[49]

The "extremely volatile language expressing group differentiation and, through differentiation, identification" used in
different periods and by different Jewish individuals or groups
sometimes masks affinities and the actual historical relationships involved.[50] Paul is associated with these other evangelists
through their common messianic convictions, though he parts
ways with them over what will turn out to be a crucial question — the inclusion of Gentile women and men in the "true
Israel," the eschatological covenant. Paul was not the only one
to use harsh language as a weapon against fellow Jews. Early
Christian depiction of other Jews — in particular, the Pharisees — as hypocrites and legalists by the New Testament writers
abounds, as we have seen. It was intended to devalue opponents
in the eyes of those for whom they wrote.[51] The writers of the
Gospels of Matthew and John contribute their share of polemic,
distorting not only individual opponents, as Paul did, but the
story of Jesus' interaction with Pharisees and others during his
life and the involvement of Jews in his death.

Our appropriation of Paul's letter is shaped "certainly more
unconsciously than consciously — by the history that has trans-
mitted it to us."[52] We come to the letter having these evangelists
already defined negatively by the tradition as trouble-makers,
agitators, Judaizers, and adherents of a now-invalid, spent,
works-righteousness religion.[53] Modern readers must deliber-
ately resist appropriating Paul's polemical portrayal of the other
evangelists.

Paul and the other evangelists differ in their interpretations
of the significance of Christ for the inclusion of Gentiles. But
on both sides of the conflict were committed Jews convinced

that Jesus' resurrection was the initiation of the eschatological age. Their positions on Gentile proselytes were genuinely held, each dependent on an underlying rationale. Adopting Paul's polemical language as the interpretive lens, the others seem "obviously" wrong. But his perspective keeps us from grasping what was so threatening to Paul about them. It was because they came across so *right* to some that Paul found them such a danger. "Their message must have made good sense to the Galatians and to others," Hans Dieter Betz writes, "and they must have been quite serious about the salvation of the Galatians. How else could one understand the fact that Paul had been pushed against the wall?"[54]

THE PROBLEMS PAUL FACED

Paul thus faced two challenges in Galatia. On one front was the continuing attraction of former religious beliefs for some in these assemblies. The detachment of some Gentiles from their pagan past was apparently less than complete, as Paul's remark suggests: "When you did not know God, you were enslaved to beings who were not gods. Now, however, that you have come to know God, or rather to be known by God, how can you turn back again to the weak and beggarly elemental spirits?" (4:8–9). On another front were fellow Jesus evangelists whose presence in Galatia threatened the credibility of his interpretation of God's acceptance of Gentile women and men.

Paul's reference to enslavement, "*do not submit again* to a yoke of slavery" (5:1) links the two challenges he faced — the present attraction of at least some men in the Galatian assemblies to the circumcision preaching and the attraction of some believers to their past pagan religious beliefs. It is to this end that Paul offers the allegory of Sarah and Hagar (4:21–5:1), completing it with an emancipatory flourish: "For freedom Christ has set us free. Stand firm, therefore, and *do not submit again* to a yoke of slavery" (5:1).[55] Since the Galatian men and women had not been bound to the Jewish law, what is the "yoke of slavery" to which they were not to submit *again*? To what does Paul's metaphor refer? To what had they been enslaved? Paul's answer is embedded in this allegory.

SARAH AND HAGAR

Discovering the meaning of Paul's allegory, its function in his argument, and its persuasiveness is aided by attending again to the preceding reference: *enslavement to beings who were by nature not gods* (4:8).[56] Susan Elliott argues that the allegory has remained puzzling to interpreters because they missed the religious features of the social world of Anatolia [Galatia]. She departs from previous scholarship with two assumptions: "First, the context of the audience is at least as informative to us in our attempts to understand the letter as hypothetically reconstructed arguments of Paul's opponents. Second, the religious frame of reference for a primarily Gentile audience must be sought in their non-Jewish and non-Christian milieu as well as in the context to which they have been converted."[57]

Paul engaged in an intense effort to show the negative consequences of circumcision for Gentile men (5:2–4). He was not speaking, however, to men for whom the religious connotations of bodily mutilation were negative. In the region of Anatolia, self-castration was practiced by young men dedicating themselves as *galli*, "sacred slaves," to the Mountain Mother of the Gods.[58] The elements of Paul's allegory were linked with this Anatolian Mother goddess worship, Elliott argues.

The first of many of the story's puzzles regards Paul's connection of *Hagar* with a *mountain* and the *law* with *slavery*. The allegory is structured by the two women and their sons. One woman, a slave, is named (Hagar), has an unnamed son, and is connected with a mountain (4:24). The other woman, free, is unnamed, has a named son (Isaac), is not connected with a mountain, and is our mother (4:26).

"The inheritance of a position in the family structure is what is at issue," writes Elliott, "not the abstract concept of freedom and slavery."[59] In Greco-Roman law, the mother's slave status determines the status of the child. Paul's point is implied: If you choose the *slave woman* as your *mother*, you will inherit her *slave status*.

From within the religious world of central Anatolia, Paul's allusions to *mountain* and *mother* would have been quite clear. In fact, they are connected. The "Mountain Mother of the Gods" oversees Anatolia. Devotion to her was widespread.[60] Each city had its own local expression of the Mother of the Gods. The local Mother goddess was often invoked under the same name as the mountain overlooking the city she ruled and protected. She also functioned as an "enforcer deity" for the Mountain Mother of the Gods. In this role she was associated with the law. In Pessinus, a major cult center of the Mountain Mother of the Gods, many adherents were "sacred slaves." Some castrated themselves in orgiastic rituals of dedication to the Mountain Mother goddess.

Paul presents circumcision as an act that will create a relation to the Mosaic law in the same way that self-castration creates a servile relation to the Mother of the Gods. Just as the *galli* were enslaved to the Mother goddess before they came to be known by God, so circumcision enslaves the circumcised to Jewish ethnic and national identity. Paul connects Hagar the *slave* to a *mountain* to diminish the Mountain Mother of the Gods. Who would worship a divine figure who is enslaved? Similarly, he links Hagar the *slave* to the *law* to argue that the Torah threatens to replace the Mountain Mother of the Gods, enslaving them once again.

The choice presented to the Galatians, Susan Elliott argues, was not simply *slavery* or *freedom*. "The structure of the decision presents the deeper implications of that decision [circumcision] as a choice to align with the old kind of 'Mother,' or with the 'Mother above.' "[61] The Galatians are presented with a choice of mothers as a choice of masters."[62] Paul's positive option is the Jerusalem above (no mountain) and the free woman (no name) who is *our mother*, who bears children by means of the promise and the Spirit.[63] Having undermined the Mother Mountain and the Jewish law by linking them with Hagar and slavery, Elliott says, Paul offers his emancipatory proclamation of Christ's redemption: "For freedom Christ has set us free. Stand firm, therefore, and do not submit again to the yoke of slavery" (5:1).

Who Were Paul's Opponents?

The more pressing of Paul's difficulties, though, stemmed not from paganism but from other Jesus evangelists. Their precise identification remains open to debate. Calvin Roetzel outlines three options:

- they were Jewish-Christians from the Jerusalem assembly
- they were Gentile Judaizers, members of the Galatian assemblies themselves
- they were religious syncretists, Gentiles who combined some features of Judaism with elements of their own folk religion.[64]

At best, settling their identity involves a probable judgment. If the evidence points to a Palestinian origin, they were Palestinian Jews whose confession that Jesus was God's Messiah had not meant that their living the way of the Torah should end. If they were "Judaizers," they were Gentiles for whom this same confession had not interfered with the belief that they should be Torah-observant. Either way, they are men for whom acceptance of the Torah is the pre-condition of salvation.

Citing Cicero and Josephus, James Dunn says that it is well-attested that many Gentiles adopted Jewish customs and attended Jewish synagogues.[65] Krister Stendahl takes the position that these others are Judaizers: "The Galatian argument is geared toward Paul's own Gentile converts who have become infatuated with Jewish ways." Calvin Roetzel, as does Dieter Georgi, argues they were Hellenistic Jewish Christians.[66] The centrality of Jerusalem in Paul's letter suggests to Dunn that the others came bearing — or claiming to bear — the authority of James and the Jerusalem community.[67] Moreover, the prominence of the law in the conflict points to those with a heightened concern with Jewish identity, characteristic more of Jews than Gentile converts and more characteristic of Palestinian rather than Diaspora Jews.[68]

Following Dunn's reading of the evidence, I take the Galatian conflict to express differences between two wings of Messianic Judaism, the Palestinian wing associated with James and the Diaspora wing associated with Paul. The other evangelists are visitors, then, to the Galatian assemblies, Jews who share James's views.[69] E. P. Sanders captures the meaning of the law for them:

> For the principle on which the law rests is perfectly clear: God gave the Torah to Israel by the hand of Moses; obedience to the Torah is the condition for retaining covenant

promises; intentional and unrepenting disobedience implies rejection of the law, rejection of the covenant for
which it is the condition, and rejection of the God who
gave the law and the covenant.[70]

While I take the position that the others are Palestinian Jews,
my argument does not depend on their specific place of origin
or even their birth as Jews. If the evangelists were not Jewish
males by birth, they were Jewish males by conversion. If the
latter, they were surely full converts themselves. It is hard to see
how their argument would be compelling to the Galatian men if
they were only sympathizers or religious syncretists themselves.
Whether from Palestine or the Diaspora, natural-born or converts, their insistence on circumcision and the full observation
of the law it signals, is sufficient evidence they were "theologically conservative," in the sense of having a "strict" view of what
was required in observance of the law for covenant fidelity.[71]
Given that the mandates of the law — if followed "strictly" —
construct separate and unequal gender spheres, their call for
circumcision envisions a particular kind of social reality for the
assembly.

This face-off between "strict" and "non-strict" constructions
of law for Jewish proselytes is part of the diversity of Jewish views about Gentile inclusion in Israel. In the story of the
conversion early in the first century C.E. of King Izates of
Adiabene, the Jewish merchant, Ananias, tells the king that he
had the status of Jewish proselyte without being circumcised.
Ananias is opposed by Eleazar, who tells the king that he must
complete his conversion with circumcision or he will be guilty
of the greatest offence against the Jewish law, to which he had
now committed himself.[72] Palestinian Judaism is characterized

as having a "strict" view of the law, in contrast to Diaspora Judaism, which has a "less strict" view, if only to see the Torah as the constitution for the land of Israel yet not binding in the same way for those outside the land. The terms *theologically liberal* for "less strict" and *theologically conservative* for "strict," have their limitations, but they do help us place views on a continuum, as we must do. In the Galatian conflict over circumcision of Gentile men, Paul is the Ananias, so to speak, of the dispute and the other evangelists the Eleazar. The source of their disagreement is not *inclusion* of Gentiles in the eschatological people of God but what was *required* of Gentile men and women. To use the political images of right and left for Jewish positions on Gentile conversion, the Palestinian evangelists' belief that Gentile proselytes must adopt the law and live as Jewish women and men is, as a theological position, on the "right" of the theological continuum. Paul's belief that God has opened Israel's salvation to Gentiles *qua* Gentile is as far "left" on the continuum of Jewish views of Gentile inclusion as one can get.[73]

It is routine for the others to be described as Paul's opponents or challengers. But it is not mandatory that we assume opposition to Paul to be their sole, even primary, reason for proselytizing in these assemblies. Like other Jews, they sought to bring Gentile women and men properly into Israel because salvation required belonging to the covenant, or, in the spirit of Philo, so that they could lead sound and steadfast lives. In the case of Galatians, bringing Gentile women and men *properly* into Israel was a direct rejection of Paul's understanding that the Gentiles' religious conversion was sufficient. Their insistence on circumcision said, at the least, that he was gravely mistaken. But they may not have located his mistake in wrong doctrine as much as in the social reality he had created with these new believers.

Covenant Fidelity as the Opponents' Ideal

Was circumcision to be required of Gentile male converts? This is a routine formulation of the Galatian conflict. We might more profitably ask: How did the Palestinian evangelists envision the eschatological assembly?

We have drawn attention early on to James Dunn's criticism that interpreters have failed "to grasp the full significance of *the social function of the law* at the time of Paul and how that determines and influences both the issues confronting Paul and Paul's responses."[74] Dunn fleshes out the social function of the law, starting with circumcision as a function of group self-definition. As the sign of the covenant, "circumcision serves very effectively as a boundary marker between Jew and Gentile."[75]

Heikki Räisänen raised the possibility, we have noted, too, that the Galatian situation may have been brought about by a growing number of Pharisees who joined the Jesus movement and whose views reflected a "thoroughly Biblical position." James Dunn notes that among first-century Jewish sects the Pharisees especially "sought to affirm and strengthen the identity of the people of God precisely by emphasizing the law's distinguishing ritual and boundary character."[76] To emphasize the difference of Jewish identity, Pharisees took the ritual purity associated with priests and other Jewish practices as defining features of the community of Israel. They wanted boundaries to be tight, not loose.[77]

E. P. Sanders denotes the Pharisaic interpretation of covenant identity by the term *covenantal nomism*. "Briefly put," he says, "covenantal nomism is the view that one's place in God's plan is established on the basis of the covenant and that this covenant requires as the proper response of man his obedience to its commandments, while providing means of atonement for transgression."[78] The Jesus assembly in Jerusalem was shaped by the covenantal nomism of Peter and James. The praxis of everyday living constituted by Torah-obedience remained in place.[79] In some way James accommodated the teaching of Jesus and his messianic mission within the sphere of traditional Judaism.[80] The requirements of covenant fidelity remained the same. Those who proclaimed the risen Jesus did so living a Jewish lifestyle constructed by the Torah.[81] For Gentile outsiders to share in Israel's salvation, therefore, they must become Jewish men and women living in fidelity to the Torah.

Covenantal nomism describes the religion known by Jesus and Paul and the other Jews before the destruction of the Temple. Antinomianism, Alan Segal says, would have been an almost inconceivable religious or political position for first-century Jews, especially for Palestinian Jews, "since the Torah was both a divine law and also, for those living in Judaea, the law of the land, its earthly constitution."[82] Segal emphasizes that this did not mean that all Jewish practice and belief in the law was uniform. Nonetheless, these two ideas — belonging to the covenant and living the way of the Torah — would have seemed unbreakable to most Jews.

"According to the opponents' theology," Hans Dieter Betz writes, "Christian existence takes place within the terms of the Jewish Torah covenant."[83] Their call for circumcision signals the "normal" Pharisaic expectations for Gentile converts:

- a full proselyte was committed to adopt the Jewish life as a whole;

- "to do the works of the law" meant to abide by everything in the book of the law;
- the Jewish way of life was a total way of life.[84]

Circumcision signaled that for the Palestinian evangelists works of the law were normative for sharing in Israel's salvation.[85] "Works" were not limited to the culturally significant practices, such as Sabbath worship and food laws. Gentile women and men were asked to take on "a whole way of life, a complete assimilation and absorption of any distinctively Gentile identity into the status of Jewish proselyte.... "[86]

James Dunn identifies these Jesus evangelists with the Jewish zealots who wanted "to draw the boundary line sharply and clearly between the people of the covenant so as to exclude those not belonging to Israel" and to convert the Gentiles "not simply to Judaism but to Judaism as they understood it."[87] The evangelists would have numerous strongly worded biblical texts to confirm their position, among them:

- "Every male among you shall be circumcised.... Any uncircumcised male...has broken my covenant" (Gen. 17:10, 14).
- "You shall keep all my statutes, and all my ordinances..." (Lev. 19:37).
- "You must neither add anything to what I command you nor take away anything from it but keep the commandments of the LORD your God with which I am charging you" (Deut. 4:2).
- "You must follow exactly the path that the LORD your God has commanded you..." (Deut 5:33).
- "See, I am setting before you today a blessing and a curse: the blessing, if you obey the commandments of the LORD

your God that I am commanding you today; and the curse, if you do not obey the commandments of the Lord your God but turn from the way that I am commanding you to-day, to follow other gods that you have not known" (Deut. 11:26–28).

Given their insistence on God's command given to Abraham, Paul's challengers were likely motivated by what they viewed as the requirement of covenant fidelity and a distinctively Jewish way of life. Against the massive weight and clear authority of scripture and tradition, Paul had appeal only to his personal rev-elatory experience. He will argue, from that foundational reality, for a community characterized by the absence of difference.

Chapter Four

WOMEN IN THE
GALATIAN ASSEMBLIES

WHAT DID THE GENTILE WOMEN of Galatia think about the circumcision preaching? What is curious is not the question but its absence in the interpretive tradition. Male theologians and exegetes, situated in patriarchal cultures and a patriarchal church, have not generally considered the subject of women to be of interest or relevance. Gender questions and analysis are relatively new in biblical studies and, for some, still remain on the periphery of interpretive concerns. Because of the literary invisibility of women in Paul's letter, it was easy for readers to take into consideration only the more visible figures, namely, Paul and the opposing evangelists. Readers also mistook the literary invisibility of women for their historical irrelevance.[1]

Without interest in or openness to the subject of women, it was unlikely that the gender implications of the sign of circumcision and the difference in Torah-observance for women and men would be noticed. Christian misunderstanding of "works of the law" as a religious legalism further diminished the likelihood that the gender implications of Torah-observance and the Galatian conflict would surface.

To locate Gentile women in the dynamics of the Galatian conflict demands a threefold strategy: (1) reconnecting Paul's theological terms to their historical contexts, (2) rejecting the supersessionist understanding of faith and works, and (3) off-setting the androcentrism of the tradition by moving women into the center of our perspective. The positions that Paul and the other evangelists took on the Gentiles then begin to look quite different. Once the supersessionism and androcentrism embedded in the ways of reading Galatians are cleared away, Paul's terms and argument begin to suggest the real historical situation in which he and others were engaged.

What salient features of the historical situation do we have in mind? We have taken the view that the evangelists stand at opposing poles theologically on how (not whether) Gentile women and men should be included in Christ-confessing communities. The evidence seems strongly to point to Paul's challengers as Torah-observant Jewish disciples of Jesus from Palestine, perhaps even from the Jerusalem church of James. To describe them as "theologically conservative," as we have, is to anticipate how they would think of the covenant law. It is not the same as the pejorative accusation of "legalistic works-righteousness." While Jews believed that God had given the law, and obeying it was common practice, there was still a range of interpretation and performance, from strict to not-so-strict. Palestinian and Diaspora Judaisms differ on both interpretation and performance, with Palestinian Judaism being strict in both respects. There are gender implications of the strict and not-so-strict positions on the law. We have also appropriated Dunn's judgment that the baptismal confession "implies a *radically reshaped social world* as viewed from a Christian perspective."[2] What it shows, he says, is that distinctions that give privileged status to some persons are abolished. But where most in the exegetical tradition begin and end their discussion of gender at Galatians 3:28, we have drawn attention to the fact that acceptance of circumcision would bear direct consequences for the assemblies and the relations of members within them. Once the Galatian dispute is seen to be over terms of membership, the question of women arises easily.

What exactly was at stake for the Gentile women? To answer this question and to situate the Galatian women, in this chapter we will:

- outline the specific situation of women in the Torah and in Palestinian Jewish communities

- contrast this with the rapidly evolving mores of women in the larger Greco-Roman milieu

- show how the situation of women in the Diaspora reflected similar trends and tensions

- characterize ways in which the Galatian women and Paul would have been affected by the circumcision preaching.

GENDER AND TORAH

As an "identity marker," the sign of circumcision creates a boundary around the people of Israel, separating members of the covenant from outsiders to it. Exclusivism was part and parcel of Judaism, as E. P. Sanders notes.[3] At the center of its self-understanding is the belief that God had set Israel apart by giving the Moses the law and requiring obedience to it. Living the way of the Torah was the condition for fidelity to the God of Israel. Theologically fulfillment of Torah met the criterion for righteousness. The "righteous Israelite" is the obedient one. Socially, its performance created the distinctive identity of Jews as a people and nation, even as a nation ruled by another. The sin of Gentiles was not their violation of the covenant demands, for they were not obligated to live the way of the Torah, but failure to worship the one true God. Jews differed from one another in their views of the status of Gentiles. At minimum, it was agreed that, while outside God's covenant with Israel, Gentiles were not outside the scope of God's grace. In the images of Israel's eschatological hopes, Gentiles were expected to come to true belief and worship in the last days.[4]

Galatians interpreters have focused almost exclusively on this insider-outsider dimension of the law, most particularly, as non-Jews themselves, to highlight Paul's view that Gentiles are now accepted by God without observance of the Jewish law. But to grasp more fully the dynamics of the conflict in the Galatian assemblies requires attention to an even more immediate social function of the law: it separates insiders from each other. The function of the law is inescapably bound up with gender. "Works of the law" denotes "living as a Jew," as James Dunn and E. P. Sanders have emphasized; but there is no generic living as a Jew. The law is gender-specific. Formulated from a male perspective, the law marks the rights, prerogatives, and obligations of men.[5]

The community is divided by gender in the first command given to Abraham. The sign of the covenant is male circumcision (Gen. 17:10–14). Males are full members of the covenant community. References to the "people" Israel refer to a community of males: "So Moses went down from the mountain to the people.... And he said to the people, 'Be ready by the third day; do not go near a woman" (Exod. 19:14–15).[6] Women were considered part of Israel, of course, but not independently. They share in the covenant through relations of dependence on their fathers, husbands, brothers, sons.

Gender difference in covenant membership reinforced the inferiority of women in relation to men. There are periodic affirmations of women's equality with men — such as the priestly writer's, "So God created humankind in his image... male and female he created them" — and portrayals of women's freedom and power. But the dominant view of the biblical writers assumes female inferiority. Biblical law portrays women as minors, dependent and inferior. More often than not, they are depicted as the property of men, as in the Decalogue imperative to male heads of households not to covet "your neighbor's house, your neighbor's wife, or male or female slave, or ox, or donkey, or anything else that belongs to your neighbor" (Ex. 20:17). *Persons* have rights and obligations. *Property* has neither.

One of the chief aims of biblical law, Phyllis Bird notes, is to assure the survival of the family as the basic unit of society. The law is formulated with the interests of the family in mind, interests identified with the male head of the family. Laws concern his rights and duties in relation to those of other men and their property. Laws are addressed to men. Property laws include those governing a wife or daughter's sexuality. A wife's sexuality was regarded as the exclusive property of her husband. Laws concerning the virginity of a bride, rape, and adultery do not concern violation of a woman's person or rights but property rights of her father or husband.

The hallmark of Judaism, as E. P. Sanders points out, is its "emphasis on correct action in every sphere of life, technically called 'orthopraxy'...."[7] He divides the law into two parts, those laws governing human relations with God and those governing relations among humans. Fundamental to the command to worship God and Jewish piety was the recitation of the Shema, "Hear, O Israel, the Lord your God, the Lord is one; and you shall love the Lord your God with all your heart, and with all your soul, and with all your might" (Deut. 6:4–5) and study of the law.[8]

By allowing or restricting its full observance, the Torah creates and maintains separate and unequal spheres for women and men.[9] Unlike men, who were obliged to obey "the whole law," women were obligated to obey only laws pertaining specifically to women. Religious prerogatives — as attested in the literary tradition of Judaism — were *male* prerogatives. The Torah's priestly code is a striking example of androcentrism. Jacob Neusner notes that, "Women in the priestly perspective on the holy life are excluded from centers of holiness. They cannot enter the sensitive domain of the cult, cannot perform the cultic service, and cannot participate even in the cultic liturgy."[10] Even the structure of the Jerusalem Temple symbolized the subordinate sphere of women. Four courts were designed in concentric circles around the innermost sanctuary, the Holy of Holies, ensuring maximum protection of the sanctuary from defilement. The Court of Priests is next to the Holy Place, followed by the Court of Israelites (men) and the Court of Women. The only court farther away from the Holy of Holies was the Court of Gentiles.[11]

As we have seen, the sign of covenant membership is the first of laws to exclude women from the public world of males, including the religious cult. Religious law is addressed only to men and only men were required, as Phyllis Bird notes, to attend the three pilgrim feasts, the primary communal religious acts of Israel.[12] Women also suffered "religious disability," she writes, by virtue of purity laws, which kept women from cultic activity because of events occasioning impurity, such as childbirth and menstruation.

The Mishnah, a second-century Jewish compilation of oral teaching, envisions an ideal Israel as a priestly nation set apart from other nations. Like the Torah, much of its instruction concerns women. Prescriptive rather than descriptive, the Mishnah provides glimpses of how at least one group of second-century male Jews — the rabbis — conceived of how women should live. It is not a historical source for Judaism as it actually existed then or earlier, nor for the actual lives of Jewish women. But the rabbis considered their teaching on women and Torah-observance to be grounded in the Torah. Drawing on the work of Judith Romney Wegner, Sheila Briggs provides a good characterization of its perspective: "The Mishnah concerned itself with a taxonomy of women, and this taxonomy was determined and limited to one consideration: the relationship of women, indeed preeminently of their sexuality and reproductive activities, to men."[13]

Further, according to the rabbinic view, only three precepts of the Torah obligated Jewish women.[14] The three positive commandments specifically incumbent on women were separating a piece of dough from the kneading bowl to give to the priests at Hallah, lighting the Sabbath candles, and upholding the laws of Family Purity. Other commandments requiring performance at specific times were not obligatory for women, presumably because they might interfere with household duties.

The rabbinic framers of the Mishnah took from the Torah what appeared an obvious conclusion: "God excludes women from cultic rites because these are the province of men."[15] The Torah provided the precedents for the Mishnaic view that "women simply do not count as full members of the community. Minors, slaves, and even foreigners (proselytes) can outgrow or otherwise overcome their respective handicaps and qualify as full Israelites; a woman never can."[16] Israelite-born women ranked not only below Israelite males but also below male converts who acquired the status of Israelite males by conversion.

Their situation, probably followed in Palestinian messianic Judaism, differed markedly from that of Greco-Roman women of the period.

Gentile women and men who became full proselytes *became* Jewish women and men. This affiliation with the people of Israel was civic and political as well as religious. Bound now by covenant law, they were obligated to take on the total Jewish way of life.[17] Their observance as men and as women followed the gendered dictates of the law. To Torah-observant Jesus-followers, the nongendered, inclusionary practice of the Diaspora assemblies must have seemed scandalous, even libertine.

GRECO-ROMAN WOMEN

Jewish conversion by women took place in a Greco-Roman milieu marked by recent changes in female mores. Although the hierarchical pattern of the Hellenistic patriarchal family was deeply entrenched in law and custom, in practice there were opportunities for women to break through this pattern, not to say women who broke the pattern completely. [18] Indeed, historians of the ancient world note the emergence of what they have designated the "new" woman or the "new" wife. In the late Roman Republic and early Empire, the new wife "was one whose social life was reported to have been pursued at the expense of family responsibilities that included the complex running of the household."[19] The new social mores embraced by at least some women in the first century C.E. included illicit sexual liaisons that violated accepted norms of marriage fidelity and chastity.[20]

In classical Greece and in the Hellenistic period, women did not generally appear in public, and the public and private domains of Greco-Roman society were strictly demarcated by gender. The public sphere was the arena of masculine activity; the private sphere was the arena of female activity; and women's leadership roles were confined to the domestic world.[21] But first-century women did appear in the public domain. Engaging in activities outside the household — commerce and litigation, for example — "women of substantial means could have the title of magistrates and exercise political influence."[22] This was true of women in the East as well as the West. In the region of Ionia in Asia Minor, a woman named Phile in the city of Priene was the first woman to hold the office of magistrate. Some women were trained in the law and acted as legal advisors, conducting even their own litigation and defenses in court. Carfania, a senator's wife, defended herself in court. A woman named Claudia Metrodora held the highest magistracy in the city of Chios twice. In addition she was priestess for life of the imperial cult and held, as Winter writes, "a prestigious religious office in the wider Ionian federation. She was a powerful women in the public arena."[23]

Examples abound of women's financial independence and entrepreneurial activity. An analysis of 170 waxed tablets discovered near Pompeii reveals women's engagement in business to be similar to men's.[24] Women were active in commerce and manufacturing. Lydia, the businesswoman "from the city of Thyatira and a dealer in purple cloth," is a familiar example from the New Testament (Acts 16:15).[25] She acted independently in joining the Jesus movement. No husband is mentioned. That is the case for many of the women mentioned directly or indirectly by the New Testament writers. Women used their own money in large-scale undertakings such as the financing of public buildings. A woman named Eumachia, for example, paid for a major building in Pompeii from money made from bricks production, and another named Mami built the temple of the

Genius of Augustus. Inscriptions for public roles and offices were shared by women and men.

In addition to their financial engagements, women participated in the public domain by joining clubs. Since there is little evidence for all-women clubs, the clubs women joined were the same clubs as men, as Wayne Meeks points out. Women and men were equal members in the Jewish colony at Elephantine, an island in the Nile. Jewish women shared in the rights given to women by Egyptian law, enlisted in military units, and contributed to the temple fund.[26]

There were also more theoretical justifications for the equality of women and men. Elisabeth Schüssler Fiorenza writes that the Stoics adopted the Cynic epigram attributed to Antisthenes, "Virtue is the same for man and for woman," and the third-century B.C.E. Greek Stoic philosopher, Cleanthes, "is said to have written a book on the topic."[27] The Roman philosopher Musonius Rufus (c. 30–100 C E.) raised the question, "Should women study philosophy?" and affirmed the need for both women and men to study the philosophers on the cardinal virtues.[28] He also defended women's study of the virtues as a contribution to the understanding of the qualities of a good wife. It is important for her to know the "science of living" (philosophy), for example, in order to be a good manager of a household, capable of anticipating its needs and able to direct the household slaves. Musonius discussed the way in which each of the cardinal virtues — self-control, justice, and courage — was operative in the life of a women. Her appropriation of the virtues is an asset for her as helper to her husband. Musonius also emphasized that daughters should be educated in the same way as sons and that virtue is important in the lives of each — for a man to be a good citizen and for a woman to manage her household well.[29] He argued that both sons and daughters should study philosophy as the means by which a human being becomes good. Musonius even argued for equality between the sexes in his sexual ethic. Just as the wife was expected not to have sexual relations with her slave, neither should the husband. To the question, "What is the chief end of marriage?" Musonius offered perfect companionship and mutual love between husband and wife.

The danger, some argued, was that the study of philosophy might make women headstrong and arrogant. They might even neglect their households and go around with men. Even the liberal Musonius was concerned that the "new" wives were "abandoning their households for the philosophical *symposia* and the competitive nature of conversations with sophists and others at the banquet."[30] Not all literary figures were open-minded. In his *Satires*, the Roman poet Juvenal made clear the personal threat that an educated female dominating dinner conversation posed for him and, in doing so, revealed something of what women were really doing:

> Let the wife, who reclines with you at dinner, not possess a rhetorical style of her own, let her not hurl at you in whirling speech the well-rounded syllogism. Let her not know all history. Let there be some thing in her reading she does not understand. I hate the woman who is consulting and poring over the grammatical treatise of Palaemon, who observes all the rules and laws of correct speech, who with antiquarian zeal quotes verses that I never heard of and corrects her ignorant female friend for slips of speech that no man need trouble about: let her husband at least be allowed to make his solecisms in peace.[31]

Finally, women's roles in public worship were well established.[32] Roman official religious cults were organized into colleges, the most important of which was the College of Vestal Virgins. Women served as priestesses in various temples. Priestesses enjoyed some rights otherwise reserved for male citizens, such as the right to bequeath property and to represent themselves in court. "Women's extensive participation in both Greek and Roman religious rites demonstrates that gender was not an impediment to religious leadership."[33] A prayer to Isis specifically evokes gender equality: "You have made the power of women equal to that of men."[34]

Jewish Women in the Diaspora

Inscriptions and other evidence suggest that Jewish women had relatively elevated and respected positions in Diaspora synagogues. But characterization of their position as "elevated and respected" may appear counter to literary evidence, as indeed it is. Many scholars assume that the evidence points in the opposite direction. Tal Ilan describes rabbinic attitudes toward women as hostile and the Mishnah as misogynist.[35] Rabbinic sources "have led many scholars to conclude that Jewish women led restricted, secluded lives and were excluded from much of the rich ritual life of Jewish men, especially from the study of Torah," Ross Shepard Kraemer writes. "Evidence from the Greco-Roman Diaspora suggests, however, that at least some Jewish women played active religious, social, economic, and even political roles in the public lives of Jewish communities."[36]

It is in this context that Shaye Cohen distinguishes between *Judaism as legislated* and *Judaism as practiced*. Evoking this difference, too, Elisabeth Schüssler Fiorenza writes that "The formal canons of codified patriarchal laws are generally more restrictive than the actual interaction and relationship of women and men and the social reality which they govern."[37]

Archaeological data demonstrate a pluralism of social roles, practices, and settings embodied in the lives of Jewish women. Specifically, archaeological evidence also points to Diaspora Jewish women active in building and maintaining synagogues over the first three centuries of the Common Era.[38] As both Bernadette Brooten and Shaye Cohen argue, synagogue titles reflect women's appropriation of leadership roles and prominence independent of their husbands.[39] Debate remains open among scholars about whether these titles were sometimes honorific for both men and women.[40] But in the view of Brooten and Cohen, inscriptions offer evidence that a woman could be the actual — and not simply honorary — head or president of the synagogue, *archisynagōgos*. The synagogue president had the central responsibility for "supervising the services, specifically for deciding who should read the Bible, lead the prayers, and give the sermon."[41] Little or no gender separation seems to have characterized Diaspora synagogue worship. In the Therapeutae and Therapeutrides, the Jewish ascetic community of the wise, women participated equally with men in communal worship and study of the Torah.

The success of Jewish proselytizing to Gentile women in the Diaspora is also well-documented. The fact that Judaism was attractive to women is mentioned frequently in ancient sources such as Josephus. More often than not, "God-fearers," Gentiles who became closely identified with the people of Israel short of full conversion, were women.[42] In at least one respect, Jewish communities may have been familiar environments for Gentile women. Louis Feldman writes that the "prominence of women in the Jewish communities of Asia Minor . . . fits in with Anatolian culture, in which women played an important part in religious and civic life."[43]

Jewish proselytism and Gentile women's conversion did not stop with the first century. Women continued to become converts to Judaism until a law promulgated by the emperor in 339 placed Jewish missionary activity under the death penalty.[44] A hint of the successful nature of Jewish proselytizing is given in the strong words of the fourth-century bishop of Constantinople John Chrysostom, a bitter opponent of the Jews, who charged Christian husbands with the responsibility of keeping their wives from going to synagogues.[45]

WOMEN PROSELYTES IN PAULINE COMMUNITIES

Paul's references to biblical figures in Galatians supposes an audience already familiar with Jewish practices and scriptures. If Gentile women and men were to hear his appeal to Abraham's faith as authoritative (3:6 ff.) and to find his allegory of Sarah and Hagar meaningful (4:21–31), they would know and value Israel's story, either by way of his own teaching or by previous association with Diaspora synagogues. While the former is likely, so, too, is the latter. Gentiles already part of the Jewish milieu seem to have been further drawn to various expressions of Jewish messianism, including Paul's.[46] In the judgment of Alan Segal, the proselytism of the Jesus-followers found its audience in Diaspora synagogues with Godfearers or semiproselytes.[47]

If the synagogue was the setting from which the Galatian believers came, they may have been familiar, too, with basic differences between Palestinian and Diaspora Jewish life. As we have seen, there is evidence to suggest the prominence of lay leaders generally and women specifically in Diaspora synagogues. In Palestine, rabbis were central in religious life and a strict interpretation of the law was associated with Palestinian

Pharisaism, one that would find the Diaspora roles taken on by women hard to accommodate. The dispute in the Jesus movement between Paul and the other evangelists mirrors Jewish differences on the interpretation of the law, the roles of women in the religious cult, and other matters that separate Palestinian and Diaspora Judaisms. Like Diaspora synagogues where a rabbinic ministry was absent, in the Pauline assemblies, lay women and men led the community's services of prayer and scripture reading.

Paul did not begin women's participation and leadership in the Jesus movement. Their involvement flourished prior to Paul's ministry. Ekkehard and Wolfgang Stegemann write, "From the beginning women belonged to Christ-confessing communities in the cities of the Roman Empire. Indeed, if one follows the presentation of the Acts of the Apostles, they even formed the constitutive core of the communities...."[48] Stephen J. Patterson points to Gos. Thom. 114 as evidence in the sayings tradition for women disciples of Jesus. He argues that the women's leadership in the Diaspora assemblies reflects Paul's continuation of the social radicalism embodied in the early movement.[49] Evidence from outside the movement implies that women were even the main proponents of early Christianity. Margaret MacDonald notes that women figure prominently in the polemical critiques of early Christianity by non-Christians. Celsus, a second-century pagan intellectual, followed well-known tactics in the denigration of a new religious group by "highlighting their attraction for women and their corrupting influence on women."[50]

While Paul does not evoke the *basileia* preaching of Jesus, the emancipatory praxis of the Pauline communities embodies it. That women were prominent members and leaders in the Diaspora assemblies is shown in Paul's other letters.[51] Women are workers and leaders in house-churches (Apphia, Philemon 1:1–2; Prisca, 1 Cor. 16:19; Lydia, Acts 16:15). Prisca is acknowledged by the title *synergos* (co-worker, missionary), like Paul but independent of him and not under his authority. Several women with titles are named in Romans 16.[52] Phoebe is designated by three significant titles: sister, *diakonos* (deacon; a missionary entrusted with preaching and teaching), and *prostasis* (leader, president). There is no indication of any difference when the title *diakonos* is given to Phoebe and when it is given to Timothy (1 Thess. 3:2). Junia is an *apostolos* (apostle). Paul uses the Greek verb, *kopiaō*, to characterize his own evangelizing and teaching and that of Mary, Tryphaena, Tryphosa, and Persis.

If one reads the reference to Phoebe in Romans 16 free from the androcentric assumption that women were excluded from leadership, Elizabeth A. Castelli writes, then Phoebe's authoritative position is clearly articulated in Paul's recommendation. Castelli's description of Phoebe suggests general characteristics of the Gentile women in Paul's assemblies, namely their independence from male family members and the integration of their social identity into the religious assembly to which they have committed themselves:

> If one further notes that Phoebe is not named in relation to her father, husband, brother, or guardian — a striking silence in the text's description of her — one might well assume that Phoebe lived and acted independently from the more typical legal relations that situated women primarily in terms of their relationship to male family members. Indeed, that Phoebe is characterized only once in a familial idiom — "our sister" — suggests that her

social identity is fully integrated into her new Christian family.[53]

Were women leaders in the Galatian assemblies? Were they independently members by their own conversion and decision? Were their identities integrated into these new groups? One cannot say yes or no on the basis of silence. On the basis of consistency, however, features of Paul's other communities are likely to have characterized those of the Galatian assemblies. While Paul uses familial language associated with the patriarchal household, for example, the *ekklēsia* lacks the hierarchical social structure of the ancient household.[54] This feature alone makes the "place" of women different from the norm. So, too, do the gender-neutral condition for being in the "circle of those whom God accepts" (by virtue of faith in Jesus), and the "indifference to gender" of baptism, the one initiation ritual, shared by women and men.[55] Whether women were leaders in the Galatians assemblies remains unknown but that women and men entered them and participated in them on an equal basis seems a reasonable assumption.

Equality of membership in the *ekklēsia* was intrinsic to the truth of the gospel (2:5, 14).[56] It was grounded first in the shared ritual of initiation and deepened by the confirming gifts of God's Spirit. We take the charismatic character of the Pauline assemblies outside the land of Israel as a fundamental difference between the Palestinian and Diaspora Jesus movements. James Dunn emphasizes that for Paul the experience of God's Spirit was not individual pietism but always within the context of community: "At the heart of the coming together of believers in the churches of the Pauline mission was the shared experience of God's Spirit."[57] Created by this experience of individual believers as charismatics, the assembly was sustained by it as well. Both women and men received the Spirit's gifts of wisdom, knowledge, faith-healing, working of miracles, prophecy, discernment of spirits, tongues, and the interpretation of tongues as the "manifestation of the Spirit [given] for the common good" (1 Cor. 12:4–11). Gender-neutral, the Spirit's gifts grounded the charismatic equality of the assembly. The foundational reality underlying the social unity Paul describes as the members being "one in Christ" was religious experience — shared in kind by women and men.

While the references in Paul and in commentators on Paul are masculine — "each member has his own gift" — women were members of the Diaspora assemblies too, of course, and the gifts of the Spirit were given to women as well as men. As Larry Hurtado emphasizes, "Galatians 3:28 makes it clear that female and male believers are included on an equal basis as 'sons' and 'heirs.'"[58] Ekkehard and Wolfgang Stegemann make gender explicit in their reference to this feature of the Pauline communities: "This indifference to gender with regard to spiritual leadership of the communities apparently resulted from the charismatic equality of Christ-confessing men and women, which found its social expression in baptism. Thus the charismatic element was egalitarian."[59] Stegemann and Stegemann's point is significant: the experience of *God* grounds the egalitarianism of the assemblies. However strong his opponents' arguments for the authority of scripture, Paul's position drew on the condition of possibility for scripture, religious experience.

The egalitarianism of the community reflects the nature of redemption as the restoration of creation. As Krister Stendahl has argued, the "no male and female" of Gal. 3:28 should be put in quotes to show that it is a reference back to Gen. 1:27. It signifies that "the most primary division of God's creation is overcome, that between male and female.... "[60] Through Christ, the dichotomy between male and female is overcome and a new unity created, one not only "discerned by the eyes of faith but *one that manifests itself in the social dimensions of the church*." [61] The question about Paul and women often is whether he is consistent in his view of women or had a genuinely liberated view of their equality. My argument bypasses these questions to focus rather, following Stendahl, on the social reality of the assembly. The Diaspora messianic communities were characterized by an *absence of difference* among members in their initiation, participation, and leadership. The Palestinian evangelists' insistence on *difference* directly challenged not just Paul himself but the kind of assemblies he had established.

In a lament turned critique, Paul writes, "You were running well: who prevented you from obeying the truth?" (5:7). The "truth" to which Paul refers is the "truth of the gospel (2:5, 14), God's covenantal inclusion of Gentiles. But God's acceptance was not of an abstraction, "Gentiles," but of actual women and men. Intrinsic to this acceptance and to its validation through the gifts of God's Spirit were new relations between them. Redemptive equality overcomes the sinfulness of inequality imposed by patriarchal structures and relations. Peter Lampe argues that the equality of all congregational members was "part of the constructed social reality of the first Christian generation — at least in the Pauline churches."[62] In a response to E. P. Sanders, Krister Stendahl stresses the social reality underlying Paul's language of "one in Christ":

I do not think we agree about Gal. 3:28....I think it is a very dangerous simplification to say that the oneness in Christ of Jews and Gentiles, slave and free, male and female only has to do with "equality of access to salvation within the body of the saved, not with social, ethnic, and other aspects. . . . " I would rather stress that Paul here speaks to the specific issue of the Galatian situation, where he stresses that oneness in Christ does have implications for the life together of Christian Jews and Gentiles.[63]

"Life together" in these exclusively Gentile communities, however, is first "life together as women and men." Stendahl's judgment about social implications should be extended explicitly with regard to gender.

The truth of the gospel is, then, not simply a concept but a performative action. *Acting consistently with the truth of the gospel* is living out this equality by members of the assembly themselves. They were "running well," living this equality, now some or all are not. This, Paul implies rather strongly, is the interference caused by the circumcision preaching. Who has prevented you from living this equality you have proclaimed as redemptive?

The Threat to the Galatian Women

That the Pauline assemblies included women has long been taken for granted, but women's particular roles and situations — until recently — were rarely discussed. Feminist biblical and theological methods demonstrated the active, even conspicuous, participation of women in the communities, but in the initial stages of historical research they also introduced a new form of supersessionism — one that contrasted an emancipatory Jesus movement against patriarchal Judaism. Like any form of Christian supersessionism, this one, too, is historically inaccurate. Bernadette Brooten's challenge changed the presumptions of Christian feminist scholars: "The inscriptional evidence for Jewish women leaders means that one cannot declare it to be a departure from Judaism that early Christian women held leadership positions."[64] The participation and leadership of Jewish and Gentile women in the Diaspora Jewish messianic communities is in continuity with Diaspora synagogues rather than exceptions to them. Elisabeth Schüssler Fiorenza complements Brooten's judgment in affirming that women's involvement in the Jesus movement was less a sudden birth of something new than the continuation and eschatological validation of practices Jewish women had already assumed in Diaspora synagogues, as well as parallel to roles women assumed in the broader social world.[65]

Did the newfound freedom of women in the civil order, in newer religious cults, in Diaspora Judaism, and in the Jesus-communities "fuel...the invective of opponents"?[66] Analogies exist. Referring to the Mishnah, Ross Kraemer asks whether the later rabbinic perspective reflects a *minority viewpoint* polemically designed to counter or neutralize a *prevalent viewpoint*, namely, one held by Diaspora Jews in which women did have significant roles and obligations as synagogue members. The "intensification of prescriptions against women," Kraemer writes, "is often a response to the increased autonomy and authority of women."[67] This dynamic is similar to what is found in Christian polemic against the Jews. Robert Wilken notes that "the virulence of Christian anti-Semitism is a sign of the vitality of Judaism in the later empire."[68] Was the call for circumcision designed to "neutralize" the "vitality of the Gentile women" in the Galatian assemblies?

Against this conflictive background, what would the adoption of this "total way of life," as proposed by the circumcision preachers, have meant for Gentile women in the Galatian assemblies? The circumcision preachers wanted Gentile women and men drawn to Christ's salvation to become full proselytes. Their covenantal nomism guided their theological vision of membership in Israel. Unlike Paul, their experience of the risen Jesus did not generate a different idea of the way in which Gentile women and men would "come in" and "stay in" the eschatological Israel. Even James, the brother of Jesus, did not understand Jesus' death or resurrection to mean that works of the law were no longer necessary.

What would change about the social reality of the Galatian assemblies if circumcision were appropriated as the condition for membership? While the historical reconstruction is hypothetical, we can affirm some changes as highly probable, if not certain:

- Gender differentiation would mark:
  - initiation rituals
  - the condition for full membership in the assembly
  - observance of the law
  - participation and status in the assembly
  - adoption of leadership roles

- Relations between men and women would be:
  - hierarchical
  - governed by male privilege

- The *ekklēsia* would be characterized by
  - status difference among members
  - restriction of participation and leadership
  - the absence of redemptive and charismatic equality
  - separate and unequal gender spheres

These far-reaching consequences would accompany the sign of circumcision. The evangelists who asked full Torah-observance of Gentile women and men expected relations among members in Galatian assemblies as well as the structure of the assemblies themselves to change radically.

We know from Antioch how offensive unrestricted social interaction between Jew and Gentile was to Jesus-followers for whom the law remained normative. Is it plausible that conservative Torah-observant Jewish Jesus-followers who found this Antiochene interaction so offensive would *not* be similarly offended — even more so — by the redemptive and charismatic equality of women and men expressed and lived in the Galatian assemblies?

While it is clear that unrestricted social interaction between Jews and Gentiles divided messianic Jews from the beginning, unrestricted social interaction between women and men would have been even more troublesome. To make matters even more tense, at least from the perspective of the visitors, most of the women mentioned by name in other Pauline letters appear to be single. For the theologically conservative male in a patriarchal world, this reality would not be comforting. "The fact that in our sources the lack of relationship to men (father, brother, son) clearly predominates cannot be insignificant in a culture that defines free individuals through a connection to a man."[69]

For Paul to promise covenant equality to Gentile *males* was one thing. But to extend covenant equality to Gentile *women* would have been, to many Jewish males, quite beyond the pale. To accept either women or men without requiring that they adopt a way of living mandated by the Torah was surely offensive to the Palestinian evangelists and a major motive for them to reproselytize the assemblies. We need not suspect them of legalism or label them guilty of works-righteousness to grant the seriousness with which persons take the constructions of their world as normative and divinely willed. [70] Very likely they considered Paul — and the communities he founded — a real and serious threat to Jewish identity. Apropos of Paul's understanding of Gentile inclusion, Calvin Roetzel has remarked that, "The status reserved for elect of Israel was offered to pagans. Small wonder that some would see this as scandalous."[71] But perhaps the scandal they saw was even worse: The status and prerogatives reserved for *elect men* of Israel had been offered to *pagan women.*

Once we acknowledge the degree to which acceptance of circumcision and works of the law would change the social reality of the assembly to conform to the gendered world constructed by the Torah, the purpose of this proselytizing venture into these charismatic assemblies raises new questions.

Did the other Jewish missionaries see the unrestricted social interaction between women and men in Galatia as unacceptable, as they had the unrestricted social interaction between Jew and Gentile in Antioch? Was their opposition to "Jew and Gentile" more specifically an opposition to the equality of *Jewish men* and *Gentile women*? Did they see "full membership" of women in the Diaspora assemblies — *pagan* women, no less — as a sure forfeiture of salvation? Did they view male privilege as an inviolable aspect of covenant fidelity?

If so, then the full character and implications of Paul's response begin to emerge. The content of the "truth of the gospel" is embedded in the baptismal confession — the unmasking of the sinfulness of exclusionary difference and the restoration of personhood to those made non-persons by religious, class, and gender privilege. In using the baptismal fragment to signal the redemptive equality experienced among women and men in the Galatian assemblies, Paul speaks directly to those who would jeopardize this equality as well as to those whose membership in the assembly was so threatened: "*all of you* are one in Christ" (3:28).

Our argument starts from a simple and uncontested fact. Paul's opponents insisted that a male-specific sign be made the condition of membership for Diaspora assemblies in which gender inclusion and equality were grounded in the experience of religious conversion, a shared rite of initiation, and the gender-neutral bestowal of the Spirit's gifts. Gender is at the heart of Galatians. The acceptance of circumcision would have had a certain and radical effect on the social reality of these assemblies, first by restricting women from full membership, and second, by separating members by gender into unequal spheres. Paul throws all of his energy into a response encouraging these assemblies to resist this condition for membership, thus offsetting its sure effects.

Paul's argument is often characterized as a defense of the covenant equality of Gentile *qua* Gentile with Jew. But the Gentiles whose equal status was threatened by the more theologically conservative viewpoint of the Palestinian evangelists were women. To be precise, then, Paul's defense was of the equality of Gentile women *qua* Gentile women in the Galatian assemblies.

Chapter Five

RECOVERING PAUL — AND THE GOSPEL

P AUL'S LETTER TO THE GALATIANS is thought to be the *magna carta* of Christian liberty. But in one of history's many deep ironies, interpretations of Galatians have actually obscured the scope and radicality of the apostle's vision; and the letter has been subverted to justify religious control, interreligious intolerance, and male privilege. In this work, I have argued that reframing Galatians involves specific disentanglement from historical, exegetical, and theological misunderstandings of the Galatian situation and Paul's letter. I have also argued that a more adequate framework must explicitly address the social function of the law in relation to gender and must specify how Gentile women would be affected by the proposal of Paul's opponents. This is a departure from previous approaches and, at the same time, an extension of contemporary insights into the conflict. This framework allows us to correlate developments in the wider Hellenistic world with specific features of women's roles in Diaspora Judaism. They in turn contextualize women's roles in the Pauline assemblies, the particular features of the charismatic ecclesiology of the communities, and the egalitarian social practices and status challenged by the circumcision preachers. Paul's theological argument of equality defended the kind of assemblies he had established from the transformation envisioned by the more conservative understanding of membership.[1]

Reconstructing the Galatian dispute through an analysis of gender reveals not only a fuller, more concretely radical gospel but also its stark contrast to:

- the covenantal nomism of the circumcision preachers

- the androcentrism of the letter itself and of its many subsequent interpretations

- a supersessionist understanding of Christian origins and

- a truncated ecclesiology that allows anything less than full participation by all Christians.

The question of women is largely missing from the exegetical tradition. One reason is that interpreters have made Paul himself the "core" of his letters — all the other actors, especially nigh-invisible ones like women, pale in comparison to Paul's dramatic experiences, personality, theological worldview, sense of urgency, and radical commitment to Christ. But there are other reasons, too, and in this chapter we explore their meaning and implications for understanding the letter, the process of interpretation, and Christian community today.

PAUL'S PREGNANT SILENCE ABOUT WOMEN

The Galatian assemblies included women and men who had found Paul's preaching compelling and life-changing. If the status and roles of women were central to the Galatian conflict, as we have argued, why does Paul not acknowledge them explicitly?

This question suggests two common observations about Galatians: the first is that Paul does not speak to women directly.

The second is that he says nothing about women. Neither observation is accurate. Paul wrote to all members of the Galatian assemblies. What he says in the letter, he says to women as well as men. His use of specifically masculine terms — *brothers, sons* — functions inclusively, as still today *mankind* is said to do. Granted the letter is silent about women but the silence reflects its origin in a patriarchal culture and its prevailing androcentrism. The principle of interpretation, as Elisabeth Schüssler Fiorenza formulates it, is that "we can assume that New Testament androcentric language on the whole is inclusive of women until proven otherwise."[2] Paul speaks to women — not just men — when he emphasizes the inclusiveness of God's acceptance and salvation. *Women* are justified by their faith in Christ (2:16), made children of God through their faith (3:26), given the Spirit (3:2). Granted women are not identified explicitly in his question, "Did you receive the Spirit . . . ?" (3:2), but then, neither are men. Women are the "friends" (4:12) whom Paul implores to stay the course.

All of Paul's references, then, are to women and men, with one exception. Paul directs his harshest remark to those attracted to the circumcision preaching. This remark clearly refers exclusively to *men*: "Listen! I, Paul, am telling you that if you let yourselves be circumcised Christ will be of no benefit to you" (5:2). Why? Is it because their circumcision signals the religious privilege of Israel's election? Or, equally true, because they would have introduced male privilege into communities in which redemption has been experienced precisely as the absence of male prerogatives? Distinctions that meant everything in the ancient world — *Jew* rather than Gentile, *master* rather than slave, *male* rather than female — were no longer to have any bearing for salvation and before God.

The relevant question about women is not, "What did Paul say about women?" but, "What were the consequences of the circumcision preaching for women?" Yet the question remains puzzling. If there were significant ramifications for the Gentile women, why did Paul not address them directly? There could be many reasons, but one factor is at least partially responsible: the androcentrism of the letter, the tradition, and contemporary scholarship.

Androcentric texts place men in the center of reality, with women appearing every so often — sometimes named, more often not — on the story's periphery. Phyllis Bird has described the Hebrew Bible as "a man's 'book,' where women appear for the most part simply as adjuncts of men, significant only in the context of men's activities."[3] More often, in either testament, women do not appear at all. An accepted exegetical principle today, however, is that the *literary* invisibility of women is not evidence of their *historical* absence.[4] Emphasizing this point, Elisabeth Schüssler Fiorenza outlines an essential task: "Rather than understand the texts as an adequate reflection of the reality about which they speak," she says, "we must search for rhetorical clues and allusions that indicate the reality about which the texts are silent."[5]

Because women's invisibility in androcentric texts is the norm, not the exception, Paul's leaving women invisible is not in itself noteworthy. It is not evidence the conflict had nothing to do with women. Women become visible when they are an exception or present a problem. In Corinth, women prophets were Paul's concern, and they are quite visible in Paul's First Letter to the Corinthians. But women are not Paul's problem in Galatia. It is men close to abandoning the redemptive and charismatic equality they had once embraced to whom Paul directs his anger: "Once again I testify to every man who lets himself be circumcised that he is obliged to obey the whole law. You who want to be justified by the law have cut yourself off from Christ; you have fallen away from grace" (5:3–4).

Everyone involved, too, would have known the difference the two conditions for membership, faith in Christ and works of the law, would make for women. At the least, and at some level of detail, everyone would have known that the Torah separates righteous from sinner, pure from impure, insider from outsider, male from female. That the Torah creates separate and unequal gender spheres becomes obvious as soon as one asks, "Whom does the sign of circumcision designate as a full covenant member?"

Until recently, interpreters of Paul — both exegetes and theologians — have been male. Their interest was often focused on Paul the theologian: What did Paul mean by faith? By justification? By living in the Spirit? The historical conflict was merely background to a heroic fight — conceived to be between Judaism and Christianity — over doctrinal concepts. The operative image evoked by the terms *Jew* and *Gentile* was male, a key factor in keeping the question of what the Gentile women thought of the circumcision preaching from arising. The androcentrism of the exegetical and theological tradition effectively blocked a basic fact: *Gentile* denotes *women*, too.

Androcentric language is nominally inclusive, while language specific to males is exclusionary. Paul's androcentric language has been interpreted as masculine-specific, burying the presence of women in the Galatian assemblies even more.

Images created by language are instrumental in the spontaneous reconstruction of historical reality. Male images correspond to masculine words. It can hardly be otherwise. *Man* conjures up the image of a male. Similarly for pronouns. *He* is a male. Images are more influential at times than words. Christian theologians routinely indicate that "God has no gender" and then, just as routinely, use masculine-specific words that reinforce the image of God as male. "Seeing a male God" carries more weight, so to speak, than technical explanations of what is meant by "God."

Similarly, with the exclusive use of masculine-specific language, "seeing" the Pauline communities as gender-inclusive is difficult. In writing about Galatians, for example, exegetes and theologians refer to the "man of faith," Christians as "spiritual men," revelation as "enlightening men," prophecy speaking to the "whole man," grace as "the act of God in and through men," and the "man who speaks under inspiration." Similarly, scholars write about the Jewish community as if it were all male — in statements such as, "Circumcision defined Jewish identity." Commentators refer to "the Galatians," "the Gentiles," "Gentile converts" and "Galatian believers" as those "who would undergo circumcision."

The fact that each of these designations — Galatians, Gentiles, converts, believers — apply to *women* as well as men is missed by the masculine-specific use of the terms. The equation of members of the Pauline assemblies with males lowers the probability that questions about where the Gentile women fit in this conflict over circumcision will occur. This male-only use of the terms is not just a feature in the style of pre-modern writers. It is found across the board in contemporary scholarship, too, in statements like these:

Galatians are male:

- the *Galatians* decided to have *themselves circumcised*.

- the *Galatians* must not submit to circumcision.

Gentiles are male:

- some Jewish Christians would only allow *Gentiles* into the community by means of *circumcision*.

- the leading apostles at Jerusalem had already agreed that *Gentile believers need not be circumcised.*

- his quarrel with *circumcision* was not that it was morally wrong for *Gentiles*.

- *for Gentiles* to be full members of the People of God they must observe the commandments of the Law such as *circumcision*.

- *Gentiles* could attend synagogue services *without receiving circumcision*.

Believers are male:

- it would be natural for Gentile believers to conclude from reading the Hebrew Bible that *circumcision was required of all believers*.

- they wanted to persuade the *Galatian believers to adopt circumcision* as necessary.

Converts are male:

- the missionaries came to *complete Paul's converts* by integrating them as heirs of Abraham *through circumcision*.

- the Christian mission was one that abstained from requiring *circumcision from its converts*.

- his converts had learned from Jewish scriptures that the biblical promises would be given to the children of Abraham and that *one becomes a son of Abraham through circumcision*.

QUESTIONING THE DOCTRINAL READING OF PAUL

Through the tradition, Pauline interpreters were certain of one thing: Paul converted from Judaism to Christianity. His vehement words on the law appeared to verify the inferiority of a religion of law. His proclamation of justification by faith in Christ appeared to validate the superiority of a religion of grace. From Paul, Christian exegetes inferred that God had not only made Gentiles equal with Jews but had replaced Jews with Gentiles as God's covenant partner. Galatians was important especially for Paul's doctrine of justification.[6] His theology was filtered through the prevailing supersessionism of the tradition, generating descriptions of "the Jewish law as the dead letter and Judaism as a narrow formalism, striving for self-righteousness and heavenly merit. . . . "[7] His contrast between "faith in Christ" and "works of the law" was at the heart of a "strong exegetical tradition in which the contrast is seen as that of God's gift of grace over and against man's self-achievement."[8]

Modern commentators have often remained within the doctrinal framework of the past. For interpreters who took male domination for granted as the order of creation, the fact that circumcision signals male privilege was of little notice. Attention focused on the circumcision preaching as a reassertion of religious privilege, not gender. The doctrinal framework offered no "place" for questions about the social dynamics of the conflict within the assemblies and among the members themselves.

A range of methodological developments in biblical scholarship undermined the interpretation of Galatians as a theological treatise. Scholars' attention turned toward the social context of Galatians — Second Temple Judaism, the political import of Jewish eschatological hopes, and differences between the Palestinian and Diaspora Jesus movement, for example. "After

Auschwitz," the doctrinal interpretation would be rendered suspect by exposure of its underlying supersessionist assumptions.
Feminist scholars further uncovered the social and cultural
assumptions of the biblical writers and their subsequent interpreters. They articulated principles of reading that bridge
both past and present concerns, as does Carolyn Osiek: "To
use a feminist liberation hermeneutic means to interpret biblical
texts with the full criticism of their androcentric and patriarchal
biases without rejecting the liberative message that a different,
critical interpretation can reveal."[9]

Any historical reconstruction of Galatians requires situating
the letter in the thoroughly Jewish social and religious milieu of
Second Temple Judaism where the issue of "what to do with the
Gentiles" makes sense. Within a Jewish evangelizing movement
that has successfully drawn Gentile women and men, the issue
was not academic. The challenge of the conservative position
on Gentiles loomed large: Was belonging to be differentiated
by gender? The question requires that we "break the silence of
the text," as Elisabeth Schüssler Fiorenza puts it, and "search
for rhetorical clues and allusions that indicate the reality about
which the texts are silent."[10] The androcentric model of early
Christian history must be challenged, she continues, and a new
pattern made operative, "one that allows us to place women as
well as men at the center of early Christian history." To this
end, we have interpreted Galatians with these factors in mind:

- Paul's preaching generated the religious conversion of
  Gentile women and men

- Women and men entered into the religious assembly the
  same way

- The common ritual of baptism eliminated male privilege

- Women and men both received gifts of the Spirit

- The communities were governed through charismatic authority

- Belonging, participating, and leadership were undifferentiated by gender

- Gender equality was a primary feature of the experience of redemption

Hans Dieter Betz writes that Galatians is Paul's response "to the first radical questioning of the Pauline gospel by Christians themselves."[11] Paul's harsh polemic reflects the seriousness with which he took this questioning. "Part of Paul's outrage," Larry Hurtado writes, "is probably due to these people violating his sphere of responsibility."[12] Paul thought that the gospel as he understood it — the inclusion of Gentiles as Gentiles into the people of God — had been accepted in Jerusalem (2:7–9). Although there was a handshake of agreement that "we would go to the Gentiles and they to the circumcised" (2:9), still the actual acceptance of what Paul called the "truth of the gospel" (2:5) by James and others in Jerusalem may have been significantly less than he imagined, perhaps especially when the gender consequences of Gentile inclusion were clearly grasped by all parties.

What Were the Men Thinking?

The Palestinian and Diaspora Jesus-communities differed in their understanding of the relation of the law to the risen Christ. The Jerusalem Jesus-followers remained fully observant of the law including worshiping in the Temple. Diaspora Jesus-followers cannot be described in contrast as non-observant, but their interpretation of the law was much more diverse than seems to have been the case with Jesus-followers in the land of Israel. The tension this caused is reflected in the conflict in Antioch over the unrestricted social interaction of Jews and Gentiles.

The problem for the evangelists challenging Paul in Galatia was not the unrestricted social interaction of Jews and Gentiles. There is strong scholarly consensus that the Galatian assemblies were exclusively Gentile. But the problem may still have been an "unrestricted social interaction." In this case it was the interaction between women and men. Offended by the social reality expressed by being "one in Christ," "circumcision" signals their solution.

Why would Gentile men drawn to Paul now be attracted to the message of the other evangelists? Commentators answer this in various ways. "The Gentiles *desired the moral security of the Jewish law* as a guide through the insecurities of moral living."[13] "Paul was writing to Gentiles who were about to adopt certain works of the law, *presumably to perfect their faith.*"[14] The letter offers little help in judging either of these possibilities.

We could put the question another way: Why would men drawn to a Jewish emancipatory movement now be attracted to a conception of the covenant community that would restrict membership and reassign the place of women and men? Why would they want an *ekklēsia* that affirmed *them* as full members and not *women*? Resentment? A precarious social identity? Regret at their downward social transition? An incomplete conversion? Hans Dieter Betz puts one fact simply. Extending equality to women, he says, "was as difficult at that time as it is at present."[15]

The level of appeal of Paul's opponents to the Galatian men is uncertain. Given circumcision's clear evocation of male privilege, it is very likely that the issue of gender arose in the debate over their preaching in the Galatian assemblies.

Without circumcision and gender-differentiated Torah-observance, "women became full members of the people of God with the same rights and duties," Schüssler Fiorenza writes.[16] She asks whether resentment eventually arose against the equality signaled by the baptismal proclamation (3:28). To assume such resentment is historically plausible to the extent that Gal. 3:28 "runs counter to the general acceptance of male religious privileges among Greeks, Romans, Persians, and also Jews in the first century C.E."[17] Resentment against equality was a likely effect of the loss of male privilege, implies Schüssler Fiorenza:

> Conversion and baptism into Christ for men, therefore, implied a much more radical break with their former social and religious self-understandings — especially for those who were also wealthy slave owners — than it did for women and slaves. While the baptismal declaration in Gal 3:28 offered a new religious vision to women and slaves, it denied all male religious prerogatives in the Christian community based on gender roles.[18]

John Barclay suggests a similar answer in describing the "precarious social identity" of the Galatian men. They adopted a new social identity through their religious conversion (3:1; 2:16). But their new identity may have been insecure since Paul's departure. The dissonance that a Gentile felt on entering this new religious group, Alan Segal writes, "was as great as Paul's, if not greater, since it probably entailed a complete resocialization."[19] Now the visiting preachers had told them that the Jerusalem leaders remained fully Torah-observant and that belonging to Israel required their adoption of the sign of covenant membership.[20] By accepting circumcision, Barclay argues,

the Galatians would also regularize their position in relation to the rest of Galatian society.... By becoming
proselytes the Galatians could hope to identify themselves
with the local synagogues and thus hold at least a more
understandable and recognizable place in society."[21]

Pheme Perkins captures the negative side of conversion as a
downward transition for males:

The social status of females and males was changed by
their conversion in different ways. For women, Spirit-
filled prophecy and possession of wisdom meant an
enhanced social status that they could not otherwise enjoy. For men, with the possible exception of slaves and
the poor, the journey was more like that of Paul, from a
position of some public esteem to a lesser or despised position. This downward transition for males is particularly
marked in Luke's portrayal of the Corinthian community
(Acts 18).[22]

In raising yet another question, Schüssler Fiorenza asks why
rich women such as Phoebe joined the Jesus movement. She
describes the contrast between the standing and influence of
women in the larger patriarchal society and in the Jesus movement as "status dissonance," which "probably was experienced
by women who joined the Christian movement, founded house
churches, and developed leadership. Their leadership in the
missionary movement allowed those who were socially and politically marginal — because they were women — to gain new
dignity and status."[23]

The difficulty may lie in the dynamics of conversion itself. As
Wayne Meeks points out, the change involved in conversion is

never total. The process of resocialization "cannot simply obliterate the ways of thinking, feeling, and valuing that were part of the person before the change began. The degree of change will vary from one person to the next, and not all aspects of anyone's personality will be equally affected by conversion."[24] Identification with Paul's Christ-confessing communities would have involved significant changes, both in relations with family and others and in the personal worldview of each believer. With the demand that believers come into Israel "the normal way," Gentile men were offered a return of status while Gentile women were presented with a loss of status. How would the latter have reacted? One cannot speak for them. But we do know that they are women in a region where, as Louis Feldman and Ross Kraemer demonstrate, at least some Jewish and Greco-Roman women were prominent in religious and civic life and identification with emancipatory movements was within the realm of historical possibility.[25] Paul's redemptive message of "freedom in Christ" had attracted the Gentile women to join these groups. Caught now between competing Jewish visions of the social reality of the eschatological assembly, they were confronted by the Palestinian evangelists and a resolutely non-emancipatory competing gospel, threatening not only their own status as members in relation to that of men but the very survival of charismatic equality in the *ekklēsia* itself.

Did the Palestinian evangelists and Gentile men drawn to them desire the return of male privilege and the reestablishment of gender spheres? Acceptance of circumcision would accomplish each. Given the insight of the new perspective that this fight is over membership, such a desire is historically plausible as a motivating cause. Whatever the motivation, Paul's judgment is severe: "You . . . have cut yourselves off from Christ; you have fallen from grace" (5:4).

A DIFFERENT GOSPEL

"Except for the demand of obedience to the Torah and acceptance of circumcision," Hans Dieter Betz says of the visitors, "their 'gospel' must have been the same as Paul's."[26] Attention to gender requires we turn Betz's observation over on its head. The *social worlds* created by charismatic authority and covenantal nomism are radically different. With circumcision, nothing would be the same and everything different about these assemblies.

The Palestinian position was grounded in scripture and widespread agreement among Jews about the requirements of Gentile conversion to Judaism. James is described as representing a hardline position on the place of circumcision and the keeping of the law.[27] Gender differentiation is an intrinsic dimension of the Torah. Marked by circumcision, in fidelity to God's first command (Gen. 17:10), males would be full members of the covenant community, and privileged with the obligation to keep the whole law.[28] The call for circumcision was, simultaneously, a clear and unambiguous call for Gentile women to take the subordinate place assigned to women by the law. With the acceptance of circumcision, the present charismatic equality would become a deviant feature of the assemblies, soon to be eliminated.

The two conditions for membership posted by the Palestinian and Diaspora evangelists created opposing conceptions of the place of women and men in the eschatological community. For Paul, religious conversion generated an egalitarian community. For the others, true covenant fidelity demanded gender differentiation. Obedience to the law was now the means to Christ's salvation.

Paul's silence about women is striking for its *positive* significance. This was a conflict over *membership* and he says nothing that could be remotely construed to differentiate between women and men members. He does not go beyond the Torah to find a new foundation for male privilege.

Commenting on male resistance to women's leadership, Ross Kraemer argues that, "Only among Christians is women's religious leadership an issue. Only Christians both attempt, sometimes successfully, to exclude women from religious office and community authority and argue about it."[29] In contrasting leadership by women in early Christian groups and Greek and Roman religious societies, Karen Jo Torjesen writes that "While women's leadership in early Christian churches had much in common with women's religious leadership in Greek and Roman societies, there is one striking difference — women's leadership in some Christian circles was bitterly contested."[30] One cause for the resistance was the perception that the authority, prestige, and honor that came with leadership was "male" rather than "female." As is common in patriarchal cultures, men granted the leadership of women in the private and domestic sphere of the household but considered the public sphere proper to males. Women's leadership in religious groups risked making her shameless. Women's "proper shame" was linked with deference, submission, and passivity.

The evangelists challenging Paul evidently did not share the same baptismal confession as the Galatian believers. Circumcision would have eliminated both the equality of Jew and Gentile as well as that of women and men. Was the latter as much their intention as the former? Was their mission designed to counter or neutralize relations of equality between women and men in the Diaspora assemblies? Did they come specifically to challenge women's membership?[31] We cannot say for certain. What is certain is that acceptance of the sign of circumcision would have eliminated women's membership and the equality they shared with men on the basis of their religious conversion.

Difference and Its Absence

The Galatian conflict echoes a tension found more broadly among Jews in Second Temple Judaism. There are those — notably Pharisees but also others — who sought to protect Jewish identity by emphasizing difference. Of primary concern was the way of life given in the Torah. Fidelity to the God of Israel was inseparable from obedience to the Torah. Gentiles were to become Jews by conversion to share in the salvation offered to Israel. Other Jews — denoted variously as Hellenistic Jews and so forth — sought to downplay Jewish difference by some cultural accommodation or by the inclusion of non-Jews attracted to their lives and worship without requiring their full conversion. Geographically, these two theological stances on the law — "conservative" and "liberal" — are identified with Palestinian and Diaspora Judaisms. Paul's opponents, Palestinian Jews most likely, emphasize *difference*. They bring a theologically conservative messianism shaped by covenantal nomism to the question of covenant membership. A Diaspora Jew, Paul takes a theologically liberal Jewish position to the extreme, rooted now in religious experience and no longer in the law. He emphasizes the *absence of difference*.

The presence of the Palestinian Jesus followers forced this tension about difference and its absence into the open: Was *difference* to be maintained? "Circumcision" signals both the question and their answer. *Jewish difference* as well as *gender difference* would maintained by the Gentile male's circumcision.

In response to the very real consequences of the theologically conservative position, Paul's argument is permeated with one overarching value: belonging is not differentiated by gender. By their religious conversion, by their faith in Christ, women and men are accepted by God (2:15) and through faith they are made children of God (3:26); both women and men have received the Spirit (3:2); those who believe are Abraham's descendants (3:7, 9) and those who belong to Christ are Abraham's offspring (3:29); women as well as men are called to freedom (5:13), neither are subject to the law (3:25; 5:18), both are to live by the Spirit (5:16); women and men are bound by the same ethical imperatives (5:16–26), both are called to do the good (6:9).

Without the Torah, differences between women and men are removed. Women, like men, entered into the assemblies as persons, turning to the God of Israel by way of their own decision. Paul's single condition of membership, "faith in Christ," Alan Segal says, means the radical reorientation and commitment of religious conversion.[32] The human capacity for conversion is gender-inclusive. The bestowal of the Spirit on women and men alike validated their conversion, rendering separate and unequal spheres a dimension of the "present evil age" (1:3) and not its rightful state (3:28).

If Paul's male converts acquiesced in circumcision, they would empty the social reality of the *ekklēsia* of the redemptive experience of mutuality constitutive of the "new creation" (6:15). In rejecting circumcision, Paul rejected male privilege, protecting as he did the status of those whose membership was directly threatened by the insistence on circumcision. He did not have to *say* what he was doing for women for others to *know* what he was doing for them.

The baptismal fragment Paul holds up as a standard unmasks the centrality of *privilege* in human sinfulness. The "new creation" rejects privilege along with the unjust structures and relations it has constructed. Paul celebrates equality even while fuming at the insult of opponents active against him in Galatia. He celebrates it not as an ideal but as experienced in the social reality created in the Galatian assemblies by real women and men. Paul fears for the future of these charismatic communities, and rightfully so. If these opponents do not eliminate the gender equality of his assemblies, there are those ahead who will be more successful. They, however, will not identify *against* Paul but *as* him, grounding woman's subordinate place in the *ekklēsia* not by the law but by her creation and her sin.[33] The preference of the tradition will be the text of Eve's punishment in Genesis 16, "and he shall rule over you" in place of the text the Gentile women surely heard as a rallying call for their resistance: "For freedom Christ has set us free. Stand firm, therefore, and do not submit again to a yoke of slavery" (5:1).

NOTES

Preface

1. The designation "new perspective" is James Dunn's. See "The New Perspective on Paul," in James D. G. Dunn, in *Jesus, Paul and the Law: Studies in Mark and Galatians* (Louisville: Westminster, 1990), 183–205.

2. The Jewish historian Tal Ilan describes her work as "guided by the most vital tool of feminist inquiry — that of placing women at the center of events" (3). Sources in which "women appear as remote or obscure, or which appear at first sight to be discussing something quite different, turn out to yield much material on women" (3). Such is the case, I will argue, with Galatians. Tal Ilan, *Integrating Women into Second Temple History* (Peabody, Mass.: Hendrickson, 2001).

3. Much of the task of "clearing away" has to do with the conceptualist and supersessionist readings of Galatians. By "conceptualist," I refer to the overarching concern of commentators in the tradition with Paul's theological concepts. Taking Galatians as a theological treatise, Paul's concepts (such as justification) were treated apart from the letter's historical and social context, thus impeding insights into the effect that a yes or no to circumcision would have had on the social reality of the assemblies, and in particular, for the membership of the Gentile women who had been drawn to these religious groups by Paul's preaching. By "supersessionist," I refer to the use Galatians as a proof-text for the invalidity of Judaism and its replacement by Christianity. These misreadings are by no means simply those of the past.

Chapter 1. Galatian Disputes

1. Krister Stendahl's seminal article, "The Apostle Paul and the Introspective Conscience of the West," *Harvard Theological Review*

56 (1963), 199–215, reprinted in idem, *Paul among Jews and Gentiles*
(Philadelphia: Fortress Press, 1977), 78–96, inaugurated the "new per-
spective." Among influential earlier works is W. D. Davies, *Paul and
Rabbinic Judaism: Some Rabbinic Elements in Pauline Theology* (New
York: Harper, 1948). Major advances were made by E. P. Sanders
in three historical studies: *Paul and Palestinian Judaism* (Philadelphia:
Fortress Press, 1977); idem, *Paul, the Law, and the Jewish People* (Minneapolis: Fortress Press, 1983); and idem, *Judaism: Practice and Belief,
63 BCE–66 CE* (Philadelphia: Trinity Press International, 1992).
Among recent contributions is Mark Nanos, *The Irony of Galatians*
(Minneapolis: Fortress Press, 2001). The new perspective challenged
and reversed historical assumptions regarding the nature of Paul's conversion and the meaning of Paul's contrast between "faith in Christ"
and "works of the law." Both will be taken up below. See James D. G.
Dunn, "The New Perspective on Paul," *Bulletin of the John Rylands
Library* 65 (1983), 95–122. John M. G. Barclay provides a summary
of the history of interpretation in *Obeying the Truth: Paul's Ethics
in Galatians* (Minneapolis: Fortress Press, 1988), 3–8. An important
groundbreaking work at the turn of the century was George Foot
Moore, *Judaism in the First Centuries of the Christian Era: The Age
of the Tannaim*, 3 vols. (Cambridge, Mass.: Harvard University Press,
1927–30). Moore initiated the historical study of Judaism. Subsequent
scholars corrected his view that Rabbinic Judaism was normative for
the first century. These studies challenged the Christian caricature of
Judaism as a religion of "works righteousness." See Sanders, *Paul and
Palestinian Judaism*: "The supposed legalistic Judaism . . . acts as the
foil against which superior forms of religion are described" (57). On
Moore and nineteenth-century developments, see pp. 33–35.

2. James D. G. Dunn, "Works of the Law and the Curse of the
Law (Galatians 3:10–14)," *New Testament Studies* 31 (1985), 523–42;
523–24. Italics in text.

3. See Tal Ilan, *Integrating Women into Second Temple Judaism*
(Peabody, Mass.: Hendrickson, 2001), 1–3. Women, for example,
were not full members of the Jewish nation. As Ilan notes, they were
excluded from the religion of Jewish men by the restriction of their
observance of the important commandments of Judaism. Keeping the
commandments of the Torah is Israel's response and obligation to the
God who chose them and made a covenant with them. This point is

central to the argument ahead. Christian commentators have taken the androcentric character of the law for granted without adverting to the significance of the fact that only men fulfill the covenant requirement.

4. Of primary significance is the work of Elisabeth Schüssler Fiorenza for the historical recovery of the role of women in the early Jesus movement as well as for the theoretical method for doing so. See *In Memory of Her: A Feminist Theological Reconstruction of Christian Origins* (New York: Crossroad, 1984); and, on Galatians in particular, idem, "Ideology, Power, and Interpretation: Galatians 3:28," in *Rhetoric and Ethic: The Politics of Biblical Studies* (Minneapolis: Fortress Press, 1999), 149–73. The literature on women is now extensive. See, for example, R. S. Kraemer and M. R. D'Angelo, eds., *Women and Christian Origins* (Oxford: Oxford University Press, 1999); on Paul in particular, see Margaret Y. MacDonald, "Reading Real Women through the Undisputed Letters of Paul," and "Rereading Paul: Early Interpreters of Paul on Women and Gender."

5. Prisca is mentioned in Romans 16:3. On women and titles in Romans 16, see Elizabeth A. Castelli, "Romans," in Elisabeth Schüssler Fiorenza, ed., *Searching the Scriptures: A Feminist Commentary*, vol. 2 (New York: Crossroad, 1994), 276–80.

6. Calvin Roetzel, *Paul: The Man and the Myth* (Minneapolis: Fortress Press, 1999). See pp. 99–100. Stephen J. Patterson characterizes Jesus' own movement and the later movement as "social radicalism." See his "Paul and the Jesus Tradition: It Is Time for Another Look," *Harvard Theological Review* 84:1 (January 1991), 23–42; esp. 33–35.

7. In Hans Dieter Betz's judgment, "Paul's message of 'freedom in Christ' must have found attentive ears among people interested in political, social, cultural, and religious emancipation." Hans Dieter Betz, *Galatians*, Hermeneia (Philadelphia: Fortress Press, 1979), 2.

8. This is not always the case. There is extensive exegetical literature on the broader subject of Paul and women. See, for example, Elaine H. Pagels, "Paul and Women: A Response to Recent Discussion," *Journal of the Academy of Religion* 42/3 (1974), 538–49. What is missing is advertence to the implications of the circumcision preaching for women and, further, how it might even concern them directly. Two examples will illustrate. James Dunn writes that the baptismal confession "implies a *radically reshaped social world* as viewed from a

Christian perspective" (italics added) and that the *distinctions between persons that give privileged status to some are abolished.* While he adverts to gender in saying that it is highly unlikely that Paul "would have allowed gender or social status as such, any more than race, to constitute a barrier against any service of the gospel" (citing Elisabeth Schüssler Fiorenza), he does not advert to the *interferences* with the "service of the gospel" that would be introduced by a gendered sign of membership. James D. G. Dunn, *The Epistle to the Galatians*, Black's New Testament Commentary (Peabody, Mass.: Hendrickson, 1993), 207. Similarly, in introducing a discussion of the Jerusalem conference, Daniel Boyarin writes: "The two most obvious such conflicts possible would be any attempt to suggest to the gentiles that in order to be full members of the People of God they must observe the commandments of the Law, such as circumcision and the rules of kashruth, or any observance on the part of Jewish Christians which would *lead to a social split and hierarchical structure between ethnic Jews and gentiles within the Church*, thus defeating Paul's whole purpose." Boyarin does not advert to the fact that circumcision would create more than one *kind* of "social split and hierarchical structure." Daniel Boyarin, *A Radical Jew: Paul and the Politics of Identity* (Berkeley: University of California Press, 1994), 112, emphasis added.

9. The sign of the covenant and command is given in Genesis 17:10. See also Lev. 12:3. In Exodus 12:48 the alien who wishes to celebrate the passover must first have "all his males circumcised." Then he is to be regarded as a "native of the land."

10. Carolyn Osiek, "Galatians," in *Women's Bible Commentary*, Carol A. Newsom and Sharon H. Ringe, eds. (Louisville: Westminster John Knox, 1992), 333–37; 333.

11. E. P. Sanders, *Judaism: Practice and Belief, 63 BCE–66 CE* (Valley Forge, Pa.: Trinity Press International, 1992), 241.

12. Larry W. Hurtado, *Lord Jesus Christ: Devotion to Jesus in Earliest Christianity* (Grand Rapids, Mich.: Eerdmans, 2003), 161.

13. On Paul's theological argument in Galatians and what he defends as the "truth of the gospel," see Dunn, *Galatians*, 150–58. Also, Betz, *Galatians*, 28–30. A central element of the argument—and its verification—was the gift of the Spirit to the Galatians.

14. Biblical quotations are taken from *The New Oxford Annotated Bible* (NRSV). References are to Galatians unless otherwise noted.

15. Krister Stendahl, *The Bible and the Role of Women*, trans. Emily T. Sander (Philadelphia: Fortress Press, 1966), 33. See Sanders, *Paul and Palestinian Judaism*, 457–58. The idea is central to Paul's thought and routinely discussed. In the work of others, see, for example, Betz, *Galatians*, 28–29; Dunn, *Galatians*, 127; and Roetzel, *Paul*, 121–25.

16. See Louis H. Feldman, *Jew and Gentile in the Ancient World: Attitudes and Interactions from Alexander to Justinian* (Princeton, N.J.: Princeton University Press, 1993); and idem, "Jewish Proselytism," in Harold W. Attridge and Gohei Hata, eds., *Eusebius, Christianity, and Judaism* (Detroit: Wayne State University Press, 1992), 372–408; Shaye J. D. Cohen, "Crossing the Boundary and Becoming a Jew," *Harvard Theological Review* 82 (1989), 13–33; and idem, "Conversion to Judaism in Historical Perspective: From Biblical Israel to Postbiblical Judaism," *Conservative Judaism* 36 (1983), 31–45; Gabriele Boccaccini, *Middle Judaism: Jewish Thought 300 B.C.E. to 200 C.E* (Minneapolis: Fortress Press, 1991), 251–65; and Peter Borgen, *Early Christianity and Hellenistic Judaism* (Edinburgh: T & T Clark, 1996). Borgen writes that "among the Jews there were different ideas, attitudes and activities at work with regard to receiving or bringing non-Jews into the Jewish religion" (46). He discusses militant forms (military conquest, proselytes from fear) and peaceful forms (religious-political proselytism, proselytes by free choice), 45–56.

17. Heikki Räisänen, "Paul's Conversion and the Development of His View of the Law," *New Testament Studies* 33 (1987), 404–19. Hellenistic Greek-speaking Jews accepted male Gentiles without circumcision on the basis of the same empirical evidence as Paul (3:2): they displayed gifts of the Spirit as Gentiles (413). Calvin Roetzel corrects the view that the Hellenistic Jewish followers of Jesus were a separate group. Such an image is a creation of Luke's in Acts. There is also no evidence, he argues, "that Hellenistic Jewish messianists repudiated Torah. Rather they would have seen the belief in Jesus as Messiah as fully compatible with Torah." Roetzel, *Paul*, 40.

18. In *Jew and Gentile in the Ancient World*, Louis Feldman notes the "liberal attitude toward paganism as seen in the *Letter of Aristeas* (16), which states that pagan worship, in fact, is directed toward the one G-d..." and the "indications in Philo (*De Specialibus Legibus*

2.12–13.44–48) and in 2 Baruch (72.4) that righteous Gentiles might be saved..." (332).

19. How Paul understood what he was doing and what he actually did are two different things. See Sanders, *Paul, the Law, and the Jewish People*, 207. Paul understood himself as bringing Gentiles into the people of God. He did not perceive that his gospel and missionary activity implied a break with Judaism. But what he does will constitute a break, one Sanders argues is clearly perceptible at two points: the election of Israel and the concept of the people of God. Paul denies the election of Israel by his understanding that the covenant includes those in Christ, no longer just Jews by descent and Gentiles who have become Jews. Further, he denies the command of God mediated by scripture (cf. Deut. 6:16) that it is by accepting and following the law that one belongs to the people of God by his understanding that one enters the people of God through faith in Christ, and further, that the people of God is now constituted by those with faith in Christ.

20. That the Galatian conflict was over membership is the core argument of the "new perspective." An overview is found in Frank J. Matera in "Galatians in Perspective," *Interpretation* 54/3 (2000), 233–45. Alan Segal writes that for Paul "being in Christ" has a present, social meaning. All who are members of the new community "define a new social reality, different from the reality of both Jews and Jewish Christians." Alan F. Segal, *Rebecca's Children: Judaism and Christianity in the Roman World* (Cambridge, Mass.: Harvard University Press, 1986). A key dimension of this new social reality — its *difference from both* the other communities — is that gender does not differentiate covenant membership. The principles of membership and salvation are the same for women and men.

21. Jews understood circumcision "as the first act of full covenant membership and obligation," James Dunn writes. Doing the law was the "obligation of those within the covenant people, as that which marked out the covenant people," that is, "to adopt a Jewish way of life through and through." Dunn, *Galatians*, 266.

22. Peter Lampe, "The Language of Equality in Early Christian House Churches: A Constructivist Approach," in David L. Balch and Carolyn Osiek, eds., *Early Christian Families in Context: An Interdisciplinary Dialogue* (Grand Rapids, Mich.: Eerdmans, 2003), 73–83;

77. Lampe notes the leadership of women as evidence that this new context of equality was not just a "subjective, mental context" but a "new social reality in the early Christian communities" (77).

23. Ibid, 78.

24. Schüssler Fiorenza, *In Memory of Her*, 210.

25. To E. P. Sanders the evidence points to exclusively Gentile communities: "It is an argument from silence, but nevertheless a striking one, to observe that there is not a single passage to indicate that there was a single Jewish member in any of the churches founded by Paul." E. P. Sanders, "Paul's Attitude toward the Jewish People," *Union Seminary Quarterly Review* 33 (1978), 175–87;178. James Dunn shares this judgment that the recipients of the letter were non-Jews, a view confirmed, he says by 4:8, "you did not know God and were in slavery to beings that by nature are not gods." Dunn, *Galatians*, 6.

26. The exegetical efforts of many patristic writers were devoted to explaining that God's rejection of the Jews was their own fault. In his work *On First Principles*, Origen (d. 254 C.E.) writes that Deuteronomy "prophetically revealed that there shall be an election of a foolish nation on account of the sins of God's former people; which election is certainly none other than that which has come to pass through Christ." Origen, *On First Principles*, ed. Kenneth Silverman (New York: Harper & Row, 1966), 261. On the *adversus Judaeos* tradition, see John T. Pawlikowski, O.S.M., "The Christ Event and the Jewish People," in Tatha Wiley, ed., *Thinking of Christ: Proclamation, Explanation, Meaning* (New York: Continuum, 2003), 103–21. With regard to the New Testament in particular, see the essays by E. P. Sanders, John G. Gager, and Amy-Jill Levine in Paula Fredriksen and Adele Reinhartz, eds., *Jesus, Judaism and Christian Anti-Judaism: Reading the New Testament after the Holocaust* (Louisville: Westminster John Knox, 2002). The word commonly used for the Nazi genocide is *holocaust*. Jews themselves use the term *Shoah*, meaning "whirlwind" or "destruction." The word *holocaust* is problematic: "A holocaust, a 'whole burnt offering,' was part of the system of sacrifice in the Temple in Jerusalem." Mary C. Boys, *Has God Only One Blessing? Judaism as a Source of Christian Understanding* (New York: Paulist Press, 2000), 12.

27. Johann-Baptist Metz, "Facing the Jews: Christian Theology after Auschwitz" in Elisabeth Schüssler Fiorenza and David Tracy, eds., *The Holocaust as Interruption, Concilium* (1984), 26–33; 27.

28. Boyarin, *A Radical Jew*, 40. Numerous works have treated the relation between Paul and theological anti-Semitism in the writings of the patristic theologians. An influential study is Rosemary Radford Ruether, *Faith and Fratricide: The Theological Roots of Anti-Semitism* (New York: Seabury Press, 1979). Among helpful sources, see Craig A. Evans and Donald A. Hagner, eds., *Anti-Semitism and Early Christianity: Issues of Polemic and Faith* (Minneapolis: Fortress Press, 1993). On Paul in particular, see Donald A. Hagner, ibid., "Paul's Quarrel with Judaism," 128–50. Also, Sidney G. Hall III, *Christian Anti-Semitism and Paul's Theology* (Minneapolis: Fortress Press, 1993). Hall's bibliography (174–80) notes further resources.

29. Central figures in this recovery of meaning are E. P. Sanders and James D. G. Dunn. On the meaning of "works of the law" in Dunn's work, for example, see his "Prolegomena to a Theology of Paul," *New Testament Studies* 40 (1994), 407–32; and idem, "Yet Once More — 'The Works of the Law': A Response," *Journal for the Study of the New Testament* 46 (1992), 99–117. In the latter article, Dunn connects what Sanders calls "covenantal nomism" with works of the law: " 'works of the law' characterize the whole mind set of 'covenantal nomism' — that is, the conviction that status within the covenant (= righteousness) is maintained by doing what the law requires ('works of the law')" (100).

30. Sanders, *Paul, the Law, and the Jewish People*, 19.

31. Jaroslav Pelikan, for example, presumes "Christianity" exists at a very early point, as this remark suggests: "More fundamental . . . is the conflict between Hellenistic Jews and Hellenistic Jewish Christians over the question of the continuity of Christianity with Judaism." Jaroslav Pelikan, *The Christian Tradition: A History of the Development of Doctrine*, vol. 1, *The Emergence of the Catholic Tradition, 100–600* (Chicago: University of Chicago Press, 1971), 13.

32. On the meaning of "works of the law," Daniel Boyarin writes that "this phrase refers precisely to those observances of the Torah which were thought by Jew and gentile alike to mark off the special status of the Jews: circumcision, kashruth, and the observances of Sabbath and the holidays. . . . Moreover, it seems likely that for

many Jews of the first century, not only did these practices mark off the covenant community exclusively but justification or salvation was dependent on being a member of that community.... The road to salvation for gentiles, according to such first-century Jews, lay in conversion and acceptance of the covenantal practices... one was *saved* by becoming Jewish." Boyarin, *A Radical Jew*, 53.

33. On this aspect of Paul's rhetoric, see James D. G. Dunn, "Echoes of Intra-Jewish Polemic in Paul's Letter to the Galatians," *Journal of Biblical Literature* 112/3 (1993), 459–77.

34. As Reginald Fuller writes, "In fact, Matthew came to serve as the preeminent Gospel for the church as a whole. From the second century on, it is the most widely cited Gospel and the most frequently read in ancient liturgical lectionaries" (951). Reginald H. Fuller, "Matthew," in *Harper's Bible Commentary*, ed. James L. Mays (San Francisco: Harper & Row, 1988), 951–82.

35. J. N. D. Kelly, *Early Christian Doctrines* (San Francisco: Harper and Row, 1978 ed.), 401.

36. Jaroslav Pelikan notes that this point is a recurring theme in treatises against the Jews in the first three centuries. Asserting that "the church had now become the new and true Israel," he says, may well have "antedated the Gospels themselves." Pelikan, *The Christian Tradition*, 16.

37. On the relation of salvation and covenant, see the discussion of the Tannaitic literature (post-first-century rabbinic works such as the *Mishnah*) in Sanders, *Paul and Palestinian Judaism*, 147–83. The rabbinic perspective reflects the biblical texts. Sanders writes that being in the covenant is explicitly related to keeping the commandments, the people of Israel should know and intend to obey the commandments of God in the Torah, and obedience demonstrates one loves God — the commandment of Deut. 6:5, you shall love the Lord your God with all your heart (83). Fulfilling the commandments is a privilege and responsibility for those in the covenant (84). The covenant exists because of God's election of Israel (87).

38. On the development of the doctrine, see Tatha Wiley, *Original Sin: Origins, Developments, Contemporary Meanings* (Mahwah, N.J.: Paulist Press, 2002).

39. Cyprian, *De cathol. eccl. unit.* 6 (third century C.E.).

40. For Barth's *Commentary on Romans*, see Clifford Green, *Karl Barth: Theologian of Freedom*, The Making of Modern Theology (Minneapolis: Fortress Press, 1991).

41. Social and political power came to the church after the conversion of Constantine in 313 C.E. and the integration of Christianity into the imperial order. On discrimination against the Jews, see Dan Cohn-Sherbok, *The Crucified Jew: Twenty Centuries of Christian Anti-Semitism* (London: HarperCollins, 1992).

42. Quoted in Boys, *Has God Only One Blessing?* 51.

43. John Chrysostom (d. 407 C.E.), "Homily One against the Jews." Quoted in Boys, *Has God Only One Blessing?* 54.

44. Martin Luther, *Jews and Their Lies* (1542). Cited in Cohn-Sherbok, *The Crucified Jew*, 73.

45. Quoted in Boys, *Has God Only One Blessing?* 19 and 203.

46. Sanders, *Paul and Palestinian Judaism*, 233. Sanders writes: "I have argued that that view [i.e., that Rabbinic religion one of legalistic works-righteousness] is completely wrong: it proceeds from theological presuppositions and is supported by systematically misunderstanding and misconstruing passages in Rabbinic literature."

47. See works previously cited by Krister Stendahl, E. P. Sanders, and James D. G. Dunn. Also Alan F. Segal, *Paul the Convert: The Apostolate and Apostasy of Saul the Pharisee* (New Haven: Yale University Press, 1990); and idem, *Rebecca's Children: Judaism and Christianity in the Roman World* (Cambridge, Mass.: Harvard University Press, 1986), especially, 96–116. An overview of scholarly views is found in Veronica Koperski, *What Are They Saying about Paul and the Law?* (New York: Paulist Press, 2001).

48. Daniel Boyarin, *A Radical Jew*, 46–47. Italics in text.

49. The insight that Paul's hostile language has to do with rejecting Torah-observance for *Gentiles*, not for Jews, has been a crucial piece in overcoming the supersessionist reading of Galatians. Yet there is in Paul's Christocentric soteriology a catch-22 for Jews. As Larry Hurtado says, faith in Christ now defines the circle of those accepted by God. Hurtado, *Lord Jesus Christ*, 89. Or, as E. P. Sanders notes, the conclusion Paul drew from God's revelation of the risen Christ to him (Gal. 1:16) is that God intends to save all, Jew and Gentile, through Christ. This has implications for the salvific value of the law. E. P. Sanders, *Paul* (Oxford: Oxford University Press, 1991), 99.

50. See Sanders, *Paul, the Law, and the Jewish People*, 18–19. In *Paul and Palestinian Judaism*, see Sanders's discussion of Gal 3:25–29. That Gentiles *as Gentiles* now have equal access to salvation (457) was a position validated, in Paul's view, by their reception of the Spirit on the basis of their faith (458).

51. Ibid., 441–42. On Rom. 10:9, see p. 445.

52. Ibid., 457.

Chapter 2. Paul's Context

1. Dieter Georgi, "The Early Church: Internal Jewish Migration or New Religion?" *Harvard Theological Review* 88:1 (1995), 35–68; 40.

2. On developments after the Jewish-Roman War in 67–70 C.E., see Alan F. Segal, *Rebecca's Children* (Cambridge, Mass.: Harvard University Press, 1986). Also James D. G. Dunn, *The Parting of the Ways* (Philadelphia: Trinity Press International, 1991).

3. See E. P. Sanders, *Paul and Palestinian Judaism* (Philadelphia: Fortress Press, 1977), 83–84 and 206–12.

4. K. C. Hanson reinforces the twofold dynamic of continuity and innovation in the Jewish self-understanding of the early Christians: "The earliest Christians in Judea and Galilee certainly saw themselves as a faction of Judaism, and not a distinct religion. But Acts 2 makes clear an issue which pervades the early Christian writings: the death of Jesus and his vindication by God were the critical events which resulted in the formation of new communities. On the one hand these Christians continued to go to synagogues (Acts 9:20; 13:5; 14:1), meet at the Jerusalem temple (2:46; 5:42; 21:26), and employ the Septuagint as their Bible (e.g., 2:17–22, 25–28, 34–35; 4:25–26). But they developed their own initiation ritual (baptism), ceremony of solidarity (Lord's Supper), foundation stories (Gospels), and leadership (pastor-teachers, evangelists, prophets, apostles). Several points of contention emerged between Christian Jews and the rest of Judaism: a focus on Jesus' death and vindication, acceptance of Gentiles, open table-fellowship, and a break with conservative Torah interpretation. Eventually they were thrown out of the synagogues" (190–91). K. C. Hanson, "Sin, Purification, and Group Process," in Henry T. C. Sun, et al., eds., *Problems in Biblical Theology: Essays*

in Honor of Rolf Knierim (Grand Rapids, Mich.: Eerdmans, 1997), 167–91.

5. Larry W. Hurtado, *Lord Jesus Christ: Devotion to Jesus in Earliest Christianity* (Grand Rapids, Mich.: Eerdmans, 2003), 95.

6. Ibid., 89.

7. See the discussion of 3:13–14 in James D. G. Dunn, *The Epistle to the Galatians*, Black's New Testament Commentary (Peabody, Mass.: Hendrickson, 1993): "The cursed status is that of a covenant breaker, put out of the covenant people, a status and condition like that of those who are outside the covenant to start with (outside the realm of covenant blessing = in the realm where the curse operates)" (176). Dunn writes that it is possible that other Jews used the Deut. 21:23 passage against the Nazarenes' claim that the crucified Jesus was Messiah. "If so," he says, "the ingenuity of Paul is shown by the fact that he does not dispute the charge (a crucified Jesus was accursed by God), but turns it to his own ends" (178). The implicit corollary to being put outside the people of God is that "God's resurrection of Jesus signified God's acceptance of the 'outsider,' the cursed law-breaker, the Gentile sinner" (178).

8. Calvin Roetzel, *Paul: The Man and the Myth* (Minneapolis: Fortress Press, 1999), 6.

9. Theissen and Merz's analysis of Jesus' eschatology sketches the features of Jewish thinking generally. See Gerd Theissen and Annette Merz, *The Historical Jesus: A Comprehensive Guide* (Minneapolis: Fortress Press, 1998), 240–80. The expectation of God's rule or reign is grounded in the Jewish conception of God's "unconditional will for the good" (275). This rule is the establishment of God's ethical will, active in the present and future. It evokes a demand on the human ethical will. An announcement of both salvation and judgment, it has social and political relevance. God's rule stands in contradiction to the existing rule (275–76).

10. Richard A. Horsley and Neil Asher Silberman, *The Message and the Kingdom: How Jesus and Paul Ignited a Revolution and Transformed the Ancient World* (Minneapolis: Fortress Press, 1997), 122–24.

11. Roetzel, *Paul*, 46.

12. Daniel Boyarin, *A Radical Jew: Paul and the Politics of Identity* (Berkeley: University of California Press, 1994), 2. Emphasis added.

13. Scholarly insight into the pluralism of Second Temple Judaism is relatively recent in both Christian and Jewish scholarship. See Shaye J. D. Cohen, "Judaism at the Time of Jesus," in Arthur E. Zannoni, ed., *Jews and Christians Speak of Jesus* (Minneapolis: Fortress Press, 1994), 3–12; E. P. Sanders, *Judaism: Practice and Belief, 63 BCE–66 CE* (Valley Forge, Pa.: Trinity Press International, 1992), 315–490; and Segal, *Rebecca's Children*, 45–67. Tal Ilan discusses the shift in Jewish scholarship from assuming the first-century dominance of the Pharisees (characteristic of later Rabbinic Judaism) to an historical understanding of "many Judaisms" in "The Attraction of Aristocratic Women to Pharisaism during the Second Temple Period," *Harvard Theological Review* 88:1 (1995), 1–33; 3–4.

14. Gabriele Boccaccini, *Middle Judaism: Jewish Thought, 300 B.C.E. to 200 C.E* (Minneapolis: Fortress Press, 1991), 13–14. "Second Temple Judaism" is a neutral designation of the period and replaces the supersessionist term *late Judaism*.

15. Tal Ilan, *Jewish Women in Greco-Roman Palestine* (Peabody, Mass.: Hendrickson, 1996), 228.

16. See Acts 15:5.

17. On "works of the law," see James D. G. Dunn, "Works of the Law and the Curse of the Law (Galatians 3:10–14), *New Testament Studies* 31 (1985), 523–42. Also, Anthony J. Saldarini, *Pharisees, Scribes and Sadducees in Palestinian Society* (Grand Rapids: Eerdmans, 2001); and Segal, *Rebecca's Children*, 52–54.

18. Calvin Roetzel, *The World That Shaped the New Testament*, 2d ed. (Louisville: Westminster John Knox, 2002), 15. For who and what the Pharisees were, see also Jacob Neusner, *From Politics to Piety: The Emergence of Pharisaic Judaism* (Englewood Cliffs, N.J.: Prentice Hall, 1973), 146.

19. James D. G. Dunn, "Works of the Law and the Curse of the Law," 524.

20. Tal Ilan, *Integrating Women into Second Temple History* (Peabody, Mass.: Hendrickson Publishers, 2001), 21. In his *Antiquities*, Ilan writes, Josephus qualifies the independence of the queen's choice by portraying her as following her dying husband's political advice. On the Pharisees and the reign of Queen Salome Alexander (76–67 B.C.E.), see Sanders, *Judaism: Practice and Belief*, 381–83. For the history of the Pharisees, see pp. 380–412; on their theology and

practice, see 413–51. Sanders emphasizes that the Pharisees did not govern directly or indirectly (459).

21. Ilan, *Integrating Women*, 11–42.

22. Quoted in ibid., 14, n. 20; cf. 17 and 25. Ilan writes that "Although it is universally accepted that the Rabbis were the heirs of the Pharisees, rabbinic literature itself is hesitant in its use of the title Pharisee. This may be because the rabbis never used 'Pharisee' as a name for themselves" (25).

23. Alan F. Segal, *Paul the Convert: The Apostolate and Apostasy of Saul the Pharisee* (New Haven: Yale University Press, 1990), 98, 105.

24. Ibid., 93.

25. Beverly Roberts Gaventa, *From Darkness to Light: Aspects of Conversion in the New Testament* (Philadelphia: Fortress Press, 1986), 26.

26. Segal, *Paul*, 93. As E. P. Sanders notes, Paul's persecution of believers had to do with his zeal but not his Pharisaism. According to Acts, the chief priest opposed the movement; and it was the High Priest, a Sadducee (Acts 5:17), who authorized Paul to go to Damascus to search out Jesus-followers (Acts 9:3–9). E. P. Sanders, *Paul* (Oxford: Oxford University Press, 1991), 8–9.

27. See "The Symbolic Significance of Common Meals for Social Intercourse" in Ekkehard W. Stegemann and Wolfgang Stegemann, *The Jesus Movement: A Social History of Its First Century* (Minneapolis: Fortress Press, 1999), 268–71. Larry Hurtado observes that eating ordinary meals with Gentiles was not necessarily a problem. The objections of Jewish Christians to eating with Gentiles (Acts 11:1–18; Gal. 2:11–21) were not about food, Hurtado says, "but about having meal fellowship with Gentiles whom they consider *incompletely converted.* The issue was not 'purity laws,' but the *requirements for treating Gentiles as fully converted to the God of Israel.*" Hurtado, *Lord Jesus Christ*, 162, n. 18. Emphasis added. What "complete conversion to the God of Israel requires" is the point of dispute between Paul and the evangelists opposing him.

28. Roetzel, *Paul*, 120.

29. Alan F. Segal, "Jewish Christianity," in Harold W. Attridge and Gohei Hata, *Eusebius, Christianity, and Judaism* (Detroit: Wayne State University Press, 1992), 326–51; 328. On James and the Jerusalem church, see pp. 329–30.

30. John Painter, *Just James: The Brother of Jesus in History and Tradition* (Minneapolis: Fortress Press, 1999), 56. See Segal, *Rebecca's Children*, 112–13.

31. Heikki Räisänen, *Paul and the Law* (Philadelphia: Fortress Press, 1983), 257. On Pharisees and Gentile conversion, see Segal, *Paul*, 98, 105; Dunn, *The Parting of the Ways*, 24–26, 130, 135–36; and John M. G. Barclay, *Obeying the Truth: Paul's Ethics in Galatians* (Minneapolis: Fortress Press, 1988), 78, 82. On Pharisaic expectations for Jewish proselytes, see Dunn, *Parting of the Ways*, 28–30, 41–42, and 128–29.

32. Joseph A. Fitzmyer, "The Letter to the Galatians," *Jerome Biblical Commentary* (Englewood Cliffs: Prentice Hall, 1990), 779–90; 781.

33. Sanders, *Paul and Palestinian Judaism*; on Gal 3:25–29, see p. 457.

34. Neusner, *From Politics to Piety*, 146.

35. See the discussion of Philo of Alexandria and Gentile converts to Judaism in Peter Borgen, *Early Christianity and Hellenistic Judaism* (Edinburgh: T & T Clark, 1996), 56–59. "Abraham is the prototype of the proselyte who leaves his home [through conversion] (*Virt.* 214)" (57).

36. Hurtado, *Lord Jesus Christ*, 86–98. Hurtado analyzes the relation between religious experience and religious innovation. Paul's religious innovation takes place within the religious horizon of Second Temple Judaism, not outside of it. In *Galatians*, Hermeneia (Philadelphia: Fortress Press, 1979), Hans Dieter Betz describes Paul's most important argument as "the argument of experience" (30). Paul's convictions arise out of his own religious experience, and he challenges his readers to draw conclusions from their own experience of the Spirit.

37. Segal, *Paul*, 110. Within the Jerusalem community, Stephen and other Hellenistic Greek-speaking Jews believed the resurrection event changed Israel's covenant identity, and in particular, thought the law was no longer necessary for Gentile inclusion. Heikki Räisänen notes the influence of the Antiochian view of the law on Paul, who was there as junior missionary to Barnabas (*cf.* 2:1–14), a view influenced by the Hellenistic Jews who left Jerusalem after Stephen's death (405). Heikki Räisänen, "Paul's Conversion and the Development of His View of the Law," *New Testament Studies* 33 (1987), 404–19. The

Hellenists accepted male Gentiles without circumcision on the basis of the same empirical evidence as Paul (3:2): they displayed gifts of the Spirit as Gentiles (413). Räisänen argues that the Hellenists interpreted the law in a spiritual or ethical way and that Paul accepted this reinterpretation in his conversion experience, understanding through his religious experience that he was called to preach the gospel of freedom from the law to Gentiles (415).

38. Segal, *Rebecca's Children*, 181.

39. Ibid.

40. See Heikki Räisänen, "Galatians 2.16 and Paul's Break with Judaism," *New Testament Studies* (1965), 223–42.

41. Hurtado, *Lord Jesus Christ*, 89. Faith in Jesus now defines the circle of those accepted by God.

42. Stegemann and Stegemann, *The Jesus Movement*, 215.

43. Calvin Roetzel, *Paul*, 45–46.

44. James D. G. Dunn, "Echoes of Intra-Jewish Polemic in Paul's Letter to the Galatians," *Journal of Biblical Literature* 112/3 (1993), 459–77; 477.

45. Jacob Neusner, "The Idea of Purity in Ancient Judaism," *Journal of the American Academy of Religion* 43/1 (1975), 15–26.

46. Segal writes that "As an apocalyptic Jew, Paul also saw this rite [baptism] as defining the boundary between outsiders and insiders." Segal, *Rebecca's Children*, 108.

47. Ibid., 109.

48. "As distinctions marking racial, social and gender differentiations, which were thought to indicate or imply relative worth or value or privileged status before God, they no longer have that significance." Dunn, *Galatians*, 207.

49. The particular construction of the pair "no longer male *and* female" (rather than *or*, as in Jew *or* Greek, slave *or* free) in Gal. 3:28 is thought to appeal to the first creation story in Genesis and the equality of male and female in sharing the image of God: "So God created humankind in his image, in the image of God he created them; male and female he created them" (Gen. 1:27). On this text see Elisabeth Schüssler Fiorenza, *In Memory of Her: A Feminist Theological Reconstruction of Christian Origins* (New York: Crossroad, 1987). Schüssler Fiorenza notes that 3:28c is an assertion that patriarchal marriage is no longer constitutive of the new community in Christ: "Irrespective

of their procreative capacities and of the social roles connected with them, persons will be full members of the Christian movement in and through baptism" (211).

50. Sanders, *Paul and Palestinian Judaism*, 514.

51. The ideas behind Christian proselytizing are similar to those noted for Philo of Alexandria: religious conversion (from pagan gods to the God of Israel known through Jesus), ethical conversion (from pagan to Jewish/Christian morality and "living in the Spirit), and social conversion (from other peoples to one people, a cross-national community). With regard to the latter, Gentile converts to the Judaism of the Jesus-followers do not become citizens of the Jewish nation of the Torah. The notion of the people of God is reshaped to mean the *ekklēsia* into which both Jews and Gentiles become members. For a comparison of Jewish and Christian evangelizing, see Peter Borgen, *Early Christianity and Hellenistic Judaism*.

52. "Many Jews, and all the Jewish Christians whose views are known to us, expected Gentiles to be brought into the people of God in the messianic period." E. P. Sanders, *Paul, the Law, and the Jewish People* (Minneapolis: Fortress Press, 1983), 18. Sanders refers to Nils A. Dahl, "The One God of Jews and Gentiles (Romans 3:29–30)," in *Studies in Paul* (Minneapolis: Augsburg Publishing House, 1977), 178–91; esp. 189.

53. Elisabeth Schüssler Fiorenza, "Women in the Early Christian Movement," in Carol P. Christ and Judith Plaskow, eds., *Womanspirit Rising: A Feminist Reader in Religion* (San Francisco: Harper & Row, 1979), 84–92; 88.

54. Pheme Perkins, *Gnosticism and the New Testament* (Minneapolis: Fortress Press, 1993), 166.

55. James D. G. Dunn, *Jesus, Paul and the Law: Studies in Mark and Galatians* (Louisville: Westminster, 1990), "The New Perspective on Paul," 183–205; 193; and idem, *Unity and Diversity in the New Testament* (Philadelphia: Westminster, 1977), 114.

56. Roetzel, *Paul*, 35. See 1 Cor. 3:16–17.

57. Ibid. Emphasis in text.

58. Hisako Kinukawa, "Purity-Impurity," in Letty M. Russell and J. Shannon Clarkson, eds., *Dictionary of Feminist Theology* (Louisville, Ky.: Westminster John Knox Press, 1996), 232–33.

59. The absence of purity as a topic or interest for Paul is all the more surprising given what surely was a concern in his Pharisaic background. In relation to Gentile converts, Alan Segal notes, Pharisaic Judaism required their obedience to the written and oral Torah as taught and practiced by the rabbis. As noted earlier, Gentile conversion entailed thorough instruction, a change of lifestyle, circumcision for men, immersion and sacrifice for all, followed by a strict and permanent regimen of purity and dietary prohibitions. Segal, *Paul*, 98, 105.

Chapter 3. Challenges and Challengers in Galatia

1. As noted, for Paul the "truth of the gospel" (2:5, 14) refers to the inclusion of Gentiles *qua* Gentiles in the Israel of God (6:16). This equality of access to salvation is also experienced within the Gentile assemblies in a common baptism and reception of the Spirit. On Paul's phrase, see, for example, the excursus on Galatians in Calvin Roetzel, *Paul: The Man and the Myth* (Minneapolis: Fortress Press, 1999), 121–25; and in E. P. Sanders, *Paul and Palestinian Judaism* (Philadelphia: Fortress Press, 1977), the discussion of "body of Christ and "one Spirit," and "in Christ," 457–59. Androcentric language ("sons of God") hinders seeing the gender-inclusive character of the Pauline assemblies as "one in Christ." This will be discussed more fully in chapter 5.

2. See William Baird, "Galatians," in James L. Mays, *Harper's Bible Commentary* (San Francisco: Harper & Row, 1988), 1204–11; 1204. In their effort to reconcile Acts and the Pauline letters on Paul's missionary trips, scholars are divided between the "north Galatian" and "south Galatian" hypotheses. See the vivid description of the people and region in Richard A. Horsley and Neil Asher Silberman, *The Message and the Kingdom: How Jesus and Paul Ignited a Revolution and Transformed the Ancient World* (Minneapolis: Fortress Press, 1997), 149–51.

3. James D. G. Dunn, *The Epistle to the Galatians*, Black's New Testament Commentary (Peabody, Mass.: Hendrickson, 1993), 5–7. See also Ekkehard W. Stegemann and Wolfgang Stegemann, *The Jesus Movement: A Social History of Its First Century* (Minneapolis: Fortress Press, 1999). Members of the messianic assemblies in the

land of Israel were predominantly, if not exclusively, Jewish (187–248). The Christ-confessing communities in the Diaspora, some argue, were exclusively Gentile (262–16). So E. P. Sanders, "Paul's Attitude toward the Jewish People," *Union Seminary Quarterly Review* 33 (1978), 175–87; 68.

4. Hans Dieter Betz, *Galatians*, Hermeneia (Philadelphia: Fortress Press, 1979), 29. The experience of redemption as dissolution of privilege links the preaching of Jesus about the *basileia tou theou* with the Jesus assemblies after his death. See Elisabeth Schüssler Fiorenza, *Jesus, Miriam's Child, Sophia's Prophet: Critical Issues in Feminist Christology* (New York: Continuum, 1995), esp. 88–96. This symbol used by Jesus "expresses a Jewish religious-political vision common to all the movements in first-century Israel. This central vision spells freedom from domination" (92).

5. The Pauline assembly "bears the traits of a fictive kinship group. . . . " Stegemann and Stegemann, *The Jesus Movement*, 286. The Jesus movement was based "not on racial and national inheritance and kinship lines, but on a new kinship with Jesus Christ." Elisabeth Schüssler Fiorenza, *In Memory of Her: A Feminist Theological Reconstruction of Christian Origins* (New York: Crossroad, 1987), 210.

6. Bruce J. Malina and Richard L. Rohrbaugh, *Social-Science Commentary on the Synoptic Gospels* (Minneapolis: Fortress Press, 1992), 175. On kinship the authors write: "Kinship norms regulate human relationships within and among family groups. At each stage of life, from birth to death, these norms determine the roles people play and the ways they interact with each other" (100). The Pauline assembly is neither the patriarchal family nor the Torah-observant people of Israel. Roles of women and men in the assembly deviate from both of these other kinship groups. Paul orders this alternative group, so to speak, around kinship by his use of familial terms. See the reference to this on the part of Jesus in K. C. Hanson and Douglas E. Oakman, *Palestine in the Time of Jesus: Social Structures and Social Conflicts* (Minneapolis: Fortress Press, 1998), 126. On kinship in the ancient world, see pp. 19–81.

7. "From the beginning women belonged to Christ-confessing communities in the cities of the Roman empire." Stegemann and Stegemann, *The Jesus Movement*, 389.

8. On *ekklēsia*, see ibid., 262–68. They discuss the problem caused by unrestricted social interaction between Jews and Gentiles (251) and the Antiochene conflict referred to by Paul (267–71). On the marital status of women, see p. 393.

9. Galatians 3:28 expresses this inclusiveness. See also 1 Cor. 12:12–27. There is no evidence from the genuine Pauline letters that membership or roles in the Diaspora communities were differentiated by gender. This is not to say that Paul was entirely consistent in his understanding of women or that he was not subject to the prevailing androcentrism of his culture. On Pauline and deutero-Pauline letters, see Calvin Roetzel, *The Letters of Paul: Conversations in Context*, 4th ed. (Louisville: Westminster John Knox, 1998).

10. Louis H. Feldman, "Jewish Proselytism," in Harold W. Attridge and Gohei Hata, eds., *Eusebius, Christianity, and Judaism* (Detroit: Wayne State University Press, 1992), 372–408. See pp. 373 and 381 on proselytism and population and p. 375 on Diaspora and conversion.

11. Wayne A. Meeks, *The First Urban Christians: The Social World of the Apostle Paul* (New Haven: Yale University Press, 1983), 207, n. 175. Jewish missionary activity is not limited to the first century C.E. or before. Its success was a concern for the church fathers in the first centuries of the church, as Lee Martin McDonald notes. See his "Anti-Judaism in the Early Church Fathers," in Craig A. Evans and Donald A. Hagner, eds., *Anti-Semitism and Early Christianity: Issues of Polemic and Faith* (Minneapolis: Fortress Press, 1993), 215–52.

12. On Jewish proselytizing and Gentile conversion, see Boccaccini, *Middle Judaism: Jewish Thought 300 B.C.E. to 200 C.E* (Minneapolis: Fortress Press, 1991), 251–65; Shaye J. D. Cohen, "Conversion to Judaism in Historical Perspective: From Biblical Israel to Post-biblical Judaism," *Conservative Judaism* 36 (1983), 31–45; idem, "Crossing the Boundary and Becoming a Jew," *Harvard Theological Review* 82 (1989), 13–33; H. H. Rowley, *From Moses to Qumran: Studies in the Old Testament* (London: Lutterworth Press, 1963), esp., "Jewish Proselyte Baptism and the Baptism of John," 211–35; and Louis H. Feldman, "Jewish Proselytism." Feldman's correlation between Jewish messianic hopes and Gentile interest is on p. 326. Also Alan F. Segal, *Rebecca's Children: Judaism and Christianity in the Roman*

World (Cambridge, Mass.: Harvard University Press, 1986). However active or successful Jewish proselytism, Segal writes, "Nothing in Judaism corresponded to the determination and effectiveness with which Christianity missionized" (97).

13. Louis H. Feldman, *Jew and Gentile in the Ancient World: Attitudes and Interactions from Alexander to Justinian* (Princeton, N.J.: Princeton University Press, 1993), 327 (Josephus, *War* 2.559–61). The following points regarding Jewish proselytizing are drawn from pp. 329–33. In Philo, see *De Virtutibus* 2.26. On God-fearers, see Stegemann and Stegemann, *The Jesus Movement*, 256–58.

14. Segal, *Rebecca's Children*, 177.

15. James D. G. Dunn, *Jesus, Paul and the Law: Studies in Mark and Galatians* (Louisville: Westminster, 1990), 193.

16. On Shammai, a first-century Pharisee and opponent of Hillel, see Anthony J. Saldarini, *Pharisees, Scribes and Sadducees in Palestinian Society* (Grand Rapids: Eerdmans, 2001), 204–11.

17. Alan F. Segal, *Paul the Convert: The Apostolate and Apostasy of Saul the Pharisee* (New Haven: Yale University Press, 1990), 114.

18. Emphasis added. On Paul's background and Pharisaism, see Roetzel, *Paul*, 8–43. In Saldarini, *Pharisees*, see 134–43.

19. Lloyd Gaston, "Paul and the Torah," in Alan Davies, ed., *Antisemitism and the Foundations of Christianity* (New York: Paulist Press, 1979), 48–71; 61.

20. Louis Feldman, "Jewish Proselytism," 387–88, 391, and 393.

21. E. P. Sanders, *Judaism: Practice and Belief, 63 BCE–66 CE* (Valley Forge, Pa.: Trinity Press International, 1992), 350. The Essenes were a sect rather than a Jewish party like the Pharisees. The sect had two branches, a monastic and fully separatist sect and another town-dwelling group (342). The monistic group separated itself from the rest of Judaism, withdrew from worship in the temple (the sect itself is now the temple [376]), and proclaimed themselves as the true Israel (354). They "hated the unjust," meaning the rest of humanity, especially other Israelites (361).

22. Cohen,"Conversion to Judaism," 31–45; 41.

23. Segal, *Rebecca*, 98; Dunn, *Galatians*, 127–30.

24. Feldman, "Jewish Proselytism," 387.

25. Ibid., 386.

26. For Philo's views on Jewish proselytes, see Peter Borgen, *Early Christianity and Hellenistic Judaism* (Edinburgh: T & T Clark, 1996), 56–59; and ch. 2, *supra*, n. 51.

27. Ibid., 57.

28. Feldman, "Jewish Proselytism," 393.

29. McDonald, "Anti-Judaism in the Early Church Fathers," esp. 239–42, "The Attractiveness of Judaism to the Christians."

30. Ibid., 240.

31. Cohen, "Crossing," 13–33.

32. On the Gentiles, see Sanders, *Paul and Palestinian Judaism*, 206–12. The perspective of the rabbis in the Tannaitic literature reflects a common view about Gentile converts in the first century: "entrance [into the people of Israel] requires accepting ('confirming') the covenant and committing oneself to obeying the commandments" (211).

33. Cohen, "Conversion to Judaism," 32.

34. Feldman, "Jewish Proselytism," 391.

35. Ibid., 372.

36. Cohen, "Crossing," 28–29.

37. Rowley, *From Moses to Qumran*, 212, 219. Also, Sanders, *Paul and Palestinian Judaism*. Referring to male converts, Sanders writes that "Precisely what the ritual was by which a man indicated his acceptance of the covenant and thus his conversion to Judaism, and the history of the development of the ritual, cannot be precisely recovered. It is to be assumed that males were circumcised. There are reports of questions that were put to would-be proselytes to test their sincerity, and at some time the custom was developed of giving proselytes a ritual bath" (206). What is certain, Sanders continues, is what was expected of the proselyte: "The formal definition of a true proselyte and a faithful native-born Israelite is the same: a man is properly in Israel who accepts the covenant, intends to obey the commandments, performs them to the best of his ability and the like" (206). This definition and expectation of one who is "properly in Israel" is at the heart of the debate between Jewish evangelists in the Galatian assemblies. Adherence to the law has implications for the structure of the assembly and relations among members.

38. Horsley and Silberman, *The Message and the Kingdom*, 31–34.

39. Ibid., 31.

40. Ibid., 32.

41. H. H. Rowley, *From Moses to Qumran*, 219, 223, 227–28. Carolyn Osiek notes the practice of ritual immersion or baptism for both sexes in "Galatians," *Women's Bible Commentary*, Carol A. Newsom and Sharon H. Ringe, eds. (Louisville: Westminster John Knox, 1992), 333–37; 334.

42. Judaism should be seen as a "religion of grace," as Christianity portrays itself. In *Judaism: Practice and Belief*, E. P. Sanders challenges — and rejects — the long-standing claim of Christian theologians that Judaism is a religion of merit and works-righteousness: "Fundamental to Jewish piety was the view that God's grace preceded the requirement of obedience and undergirds both the life of Israel and also the entire universe.... God's grace underlies human existence" (275–76).

43. Horsley and Silberman, *The Message and the Kingdom*, 32–34.

44. Segal, *Rebecca's Children*, 108.

45. Stegemann and Stegemann, *The Jesus Movement*. On baptism and the reception of the Spirit, see 393–95. See pp. 271–72 for their discussion of "Charisma as a Basis for Deviation from Jewish Social Behavior."

46. The descriptive term is Bruce Malina's. Used in this context for the first-century C.E., it is also appropriate for religion in earlier centuries. Bruce J. Malina, *The Social Gospel of Jesus: The Kingdom of God in Mediterranean Perspective* (Minneapolis: Fortress Press, 2001), 94. The temple is the center of political religion.

47. Scot McKnight, "A Loyal Critic: Matthew's Polemic with Judaism in Theological Perspective," in Evans and Hagner, eds., *Anti-Semitism and Early Christianity*, 55–79; 55.

48. Paul's understanding of what was agreed upon in Jerusalem may not have been the same as what James and others understood as their agreement. In John Painter's judgment, James did not share Paul's views about his Gentile mission. Painter refers to Acts 21:20 and emphasizes the law-observant character of the Jerusalem church. In the Antioch situation (2:11), Peter withdrew from table fellowship with Gentile believers after the messengers came from James: "Certainly it suggests that James did not believe there was an equality between the two missions which allowed total freedom of full relationship between Jewish and Gentile believers. From this perspective it appears

that, although James acknowledged a mission to the Gentiles that did not involve full law observance, he did not regard that mission to be on equal terms to the Jerusalem mission and consequently full fellowship between the two missions was not possible." John Painter, "Who was James? Footprints as a Means of Identification," in Bruce Chilton and Jacob Neusner, eds., *The Brother of Jesus: James the Just and His Mission* (Louisville: Westminster John Knox, 2001), 10–65; 32.

49. James Dunn points to the views of J. L. Martyn in this regard. Martyn, he says, "sees such a line of exegesis as in effect a surrender to the theology of the other missionaries (whom he calls 'the Teachers') whereas the cross has meant for Paul a quantum shift into a wholly new and different perspective (especially 6:14–15)." James D. G. Dunn, "Echoes of Intra-Jewish Polemic in Paul's Letter to the Galatians," *Journal of Biblical Literature* 112/3 (1993), 459–77; 477. He refers to J. L. Martyn, "Events in Galatia," in Jouette M. Bassler, editor, *Pauline Theology*: Vol. 1: *Thessalonians, Philippians, Galatians, Philemon* (Minneapolis: Fortress Press, 1991), 160–79.

50. McKnight, "A Loyal Critic," 56.

51. "Pharisee" became synonymous with "hypocrite" in the Christian tradition. The New Testament portrayal of Pharisees is now recognized as polemical and historically inaccurate. See Jacob Neusner, *From Politics to Piety: The Emergence of Pharisaic Judaism* (Englewood Cliffs: Prentice Hall, 1973), and idem, *Judaism in the Beginning of Christianity* (Philadelphia: Fortress Press, 1984). Knowledge of this inaccuracy has not keep the caricature from being given historical credibility in homilies and classrooms.

52. Dieter Lührmann, *Galatians: A Continental Commentary*, trans. O. C. Dean, Jr. (Minneapolis: Fortress Press, 1992 ed.), 5. The text "comes with" the reading given to it by Martin Luther, for example. In addition to this history, "the interpretation must take into consideration what associations we make with the great key words of the letter, such as faith, law, righteousness, freedom" (6).

53. The term *Judaizers* took on a derogatory meaning in the Christian tradition of those trying to force the law on others. This pejorative sense continues. For example, J. N. D. Kelly describes the second-century Ebionites as a Judaizing Christianity whose interest was "*saddling* the Church with full observance of the law." J. N. D. Kelly, *Early Christian Doctrines* (San Francisco: Harper and Row, 1978

ed.), 139., emphasis added. In its first-century context the term has a non-pejorative meaning, as James Dunn points out: "'To judaize' was a quite familiar expression, meaning 'to adopt a (characteristically) Jewish way of life'." Dunn, *Galatians*, 129. The use of neutral designations — the others, the visiting evangelists, the circumcision preachers — offsets the supersessionist tradition.

54. Betz, *Galatians*, 7.

55. Emphasis added. Understanding both the allegory and its place in relation to Paul's argument is important. Decoding it is a major hurdle in Galatians interpretation of Paul's argument. Among recent contributions, J. L. Martyn argues that Paul is contrasting law-observant and law-free Jewish Christian movements. See "The Covenants of Hagar and Sarah," in J. T. Carroll, C. H. Cosgrove, and E. E. Johnson, *Faith and History: Essays in Honor of Paul W. Meyer* (Atlanta: Scholars Press, 1990), 161–92.

56. Susan Elliott's analysis is especially valuable for decoding this enigmatic allegory. See Susan M. Elliott, "Choose Your Mother, Choose Your Master: Galatians 4:21–5:1 in the Shadow of the Anatolian Mother of the Gods,"*Journal of Biblical Literature* 118/4 (1999), 666–83. Our treatment of the allegory follows Elliott's analysis.

57. Ibid., 666.

58. In the Anatolian context, Elliott argues, circumcision was "a ritual with a functional similarity to castration." Ibid., 680.

59. Ibid., 661. Elliott refers to status in Greco-Roman law on p. 666, n. 19.

60. Ibid., 672, n. 41. Elliott notes that the cult of the Mother of the Gods is usually studied as the cult of Cybele and Attis. She takes both the southern and northern Galatians hypotheses and notes locations where the Mother of the Gods is worshiped in her local form. In the north a major site is the city of Pessinus, which Elliott describes as a temple state, populated by sacred slaves, "administered by a temple hierarchy, and ruled by a priest-king, Attis, who represented the object of the goddess's affection" (674). See also, Marten J. Vermaseren, *Cybele and Attis: The Myth and the Cult* (New York: Thames and Hudson, 1977). Also, Marvin W. Meyer, "The Anatolian Mysteries of the Great Mother and Her Lover" in Marvin W. Meyer, ed., *The Ancient Mysteries: Sacred Texts of the Mystery Religions of the Ancient Mediterranean World* (San Francisco: Harper and Row, 1987), 113–54. Meyers

refers to "the flamboyant Galli," eunuchs of the Great Mother (115). In the first century C.E., the Latin poet Catullus composed a poem about Attis, who in the madness of frenzy, castrates himself and becomes *notha mulier*, "counterfeit woman." After bemoaning "her" fate, Attis becomes a slave of the Great Mother (125–26). James Dunn notes that Paul's wish that his opponents would castrate themselves (5:12) may be a reference to the practice of self-castration in the cult of Cybele, which had its home in Galatia. Dunn, *Galatians*, 283.

61. Elliott, "Choose Your Mother," 680.

62. Ibid., 680.

63. "Paul offers another 'mother' as a city above the mountains and as a legitimate wife whose sons are free." Ibid., 683.

64. Roetzel, *The Letters of Paul*, 98–100.

65. Dunn, *Galatians*, 129. Citing Plutarch's *Cicero* vii.6 and Josephus, *War* ii. 463.

66. Roetzel, *Paul*, 198, n. 30.

67. Dunn, *Galatians*, 9–14. Among others, Joseph Fitzmyer and Alan Segal share Dunn's view on the Palestinian origin of the others. See Fitzmyer, "Galatians," 781, and Segal, *Paul*, 117–49. John Painter suggests their theological perspective in his characterization of James. Noting Luke's portrayal of James in Acts, Painter writes that Luke "sought to minimize the role of James because he was aware that James represented a hard-line position on the place of circumcision and the keeping of the law, a position that Luke himself did not wish to retain" (56). John Painter, *Just James: The Brother of Jesus in History and Tradition* (Minneapolis: Fortress Press, 1999). See also, Alan F. Segal, "Jewish Christianity," in Attridge and Hata, eds., *Eusebius, Christianity, and Judaism*, 326–49, esp. 329–30. An alternate view is proposed by Mark Nanos in his *The Irony of Galatians* (Minneapolis: Fortress Press, 2001). As Nanos reconstructs the Galatian situation, Gentile converts to Christianity who desire to be accepted by the wider Jewish community are disappointed to find they are not accepted unless they undergo the rituals of full proselyte conversion.

68. For "Judaizer" to be a plausible social or religious identity for the Gentiles in these assemblies, Pheme Perkins argues, it makes more sense to see their interaction with the local Jewish community as the reason for their attraction to taking on Jewish customs rather than being pushed into this way of life by authorities from Jerusalem or

Antioch. The evangelists challenging Paul — outsiders, not insiders — may have sparked their interest. Pheme Perkins, *Abraham's Divided Children: Galatians and the Politics of Faith* (Harrisburg, Pa.: Trinity Press International, 2001), 16.

69. This is the view of Frank Matera in "Galatians in Perspective: Cutting a New Path through Old Territory," *Interpretation* 54 (July 2000), 233–45; 237. For Matera's full analysis, see *Galatians*, Sacra Pagina 9 (Collegeville, Liturgical Press, 1992).

70. E. P. Sanders, *Jesus and Judaism* (Philadelphia: Fortress Press, 1976), 56–57. Italics in text.

71. James Dunn describes Paul's opponents as conservative. Saying that "false brothers" is Paul's description, Dunn writes: "But presumably they were also Christians, believers in Jesus as Messiah crucified and raised, and baptized in his name. Evidently they were much more conservative on the matter of maintaining Israel's distinctive identity and boundaries than the Jerusalem leaders, and certainly than Paul.... They saw their new loyalty (to Messiah Jesus) as an extension of their traditional faith, the new movement of the Nazarenes as wholly *within* the Judaism of the second Temple period" (128). James D. G. Dunn, *The Parting of the Ways* (Philadelphia: Trinity Press International, 1991).

72. The story of Queen Helena and King Izates in the first century C.E. is a frequently used example in secondary sources dealing with Gentile conversion to Judaism in the ancient world. See, for example, Borgen, *Early Christianity and Hellenistic Judaism*, 52–53.

73. For Paul's understanding of Gentile inclusion, see Sanders, *Paul and Palestinian Judaism*. As Sanders describes it, the theme of Paul's gospel "was the saving action of God in Jesus Christ and how his hearers could participate in that action.... The principal word for that participation is 'faith' or 'believing'..." (447). Sanders discusses Pauline soteriology on pp. 447–74.

74. James D. G. Dunn, "Works of the Law and the Curse of the Law (Galatians 3:10–14)," *New Testament Studies* 31 (1985): 523–42; 524. While deeply appreciative of E. P. Sanders's work, Dunn writes that Sanders "failed to get sufficiently inside the social situation of which 'Paul and the law' were a part."

75. Ibid., 530.

76. Ibid., 526.

77. Alan F. Segal, *Paul the Convert*, 96–105.

78. Sanders, *Paul and Palestinian Judaism*, 75. On covenantal nomism as the religion of Jesus and Paul, see p. 426. In his later book, *Judaism: Practice and Belief*, Sanders emphasized that the Pharisees' beliefs were common to Jews. See pp. 241–78. Sanders gives the general outlines of the theology held by the Pharisees on pp. 415–46. Prior to the work of Jacob Neusner, scholars tended to assume that the rabbinic literature could be used as a historical source for the Pharisees in the first century C.E. Sanders affirms that there is a link between pre-70 Pharisaism and post-70 rabbis yet also reinforces Neusner's view that the rabbinic literature is not a historical source for the minds of the Pharisees.

79. See the discussion of the two missions in Painter, *Just James*, 58–82. Painter suggests the complexity of the historical situation in a section title, "Two Missions, Many Factions" (73).

80. Segal, *Paul*, 113; and Shaye J. D. Cohen, "Judaism at the Time of Jesus," in Arthur E. Zannoni, ed., *Jews and Christians Speak of Jesus* (Minneapolis: Fortress Press, 1994), 3–12. See also Painter, *Just James*. James "the Just" or "the Righteous" implies that James was faithful to the law (48).

81. Dunn, *The Parting of the Ways*, 27; and Painter, *Just James*, 56, 97–98, 101–2.

82. Segal, "Jewish Christianity," 327.

83. Betz, *Galatians*, 9.

84. Dunn, *Galatians*, 266–67.

85. Segal, *Rebecca*, 114.

86. Dunn, *Galatians*, 267.

87. Ibid., 258. See also idem, "The Theology of Galatians: The Issue of Covenantal Nomism," in Bassler, ed., *Pauline Theology*: vol. 1, 125–46: "Galatians is Paul's first sustained attempt to deal with covenantal nomism" (125). It is unlikely, Dunn argues, that Paul's argument will be understood "without an adequate grasp of *the taken-for-granted nature of covenantal nomism within Jewish circles*" (127; emphasis in original). As examples of "two Christianities" or Messianic Judaisms (Palestinian and Diaspora), Gabriele Boccaccini compares the Letter of James and Paul's Letter to the Romans. Boccaccini, *Middle Judaism*, 213–28. On James and the Jerusalem church,

see Segal, "Jewish Christianity," in Attridge and Hata, eds., *Eusebius, Christianity, and Judaism*, 329–30.

Chapter 4. Women in the Galatian Assemblies

1. Christianity, like other ancient religious groups, developed and existed in patriarchal cultures, where a "systematic bias in favor of the male characterizes language, laws and most formal structures and relationships." Phyllis Bird, "Images of Women in the Old Testament," in Rosemary Radford Ruether, *Religion and Sexism: Images of Women in the Jewish and Christian Traditions* (New York: Simon and Schuster, 1974), 41–88; 86, n. 83. In developing analytical categories for feminist theory, Elisabeth Schüssler Fiorenza has replaced the commonly used category of patriarchy with that of kyriarchy to make more explicit the multiple and overlapping structures of domination. She writes that "'Kyriarchy' means the domination of the lord, slave master, husband, the elite freeborn educated and propertied man over all wo/men and subaltern men." Kyriarchal relations of domination, she continues, "are built on elite male property rights over wo/men, who are marked by the intersection of gender, race, class, and imperial domination as well as wo/men's dependency, subordination, and obedience — or wo/men's second-class citizenship." Such relations characterize both ancient and modern societies. Elisabeth Schüssler Fiorenza, *Jesus and the Politics of Interpretation* (New York: Continuum, 2000), 95, 96.

2. James D. G. Dunn, *The Epistle to the Galatians*, Black's New Testament Commentary (Peabody, Mass.: Hendrickson, 1993), 207. The following point is Dunn's.

3. E. P. Sanders, *Judaism: Practice and Belief, 63 BCE–66 CE* (Valley Forge, Pa.: Trinity Press International, 1992), 266–67. The status of Gentiles is a legal and theological question. The Jews perceived their own covenant and obligations as unique to them but also believed that God had created the world and made a covenant with humanity (270). See Sanders's discussion of different Jewish writers and their views (267–70). Pseudo-Philo, for example, took the law as the standard by which everyone would be judged (267). Diaspora Jews, including Paul, argued that "nature" is a standard given by God and

known to Jews and Gentiles alike (268). The rabbis developed the category of the "righteous Gentile" (269) which, like the argument from nature, drew on the idea that at least some aspect of the law for Gentiles is "written on their hearts." Sanders emphasizes that fundamental to Jewish piety was the view that "God's grace preceded the requirement of obedience and undergirds both the life of Israel and also the entire universe" (275–76). On the Gentiles, see also idem, *Paul and Palestinian Judaism* (Philadelphia: Fortress Press, 1977), 206–12.

4. Themes concerning the Gentiles vary: they will be converted, destroyed, or subjugated. Ibid., 290–92. For example, the prophet Isaiah evokes two of the three virtually back to back: "They shall bring gold and frankincense, and shall proclaim the praise of the Lord" (60.6). "Those who do not submit will be destroyed" (60:12). Eschatological hopes have to do a "new and better" time in the future with the restoration of the people of Israel and the temple. Images of the Gentiles fit into this picture — they either enter into Israel, stay out of the way of restoration, or are destroyed so they don't interfere.

5. Ross Shepard Kraemer, *Her Share of the Blessings: Women's Religions among Pagans, Jews, and Christians in the Greco-Roman World* (New York: Oxford University Press, 1992), 96–105. See also Tal Ilan, *Integrating Women into Second Temple History* (Peabody, Mass.: Hendrickson, 2001), 1–3. Women, like Gentiles, Ilan writes, "were excluded from participating in the most important commandments of Judaism. The special commandments imposed on women, however, were not viewed as a blessing, but as a curse (*yShabbat* 2:4, 5b)" (3).

6. Ibid., 50. The following points on the law are drawn from pp. 51–57.

7. Sanders, *Judaism*, 191. On the law and its observance, see pp. 190–240.

8. Ibid., 195, 197.

9. Kraemer, *Blessings*, 105.

10. Jacob Neusner, "Women in the System of Mishnah," *Conservative Judaism* 33 (1980), 3–13.

11. James D. G. Dunn, *The Parting of the Ways* (Philadelphia: Trinity Press International, 1991), 39.

12. Bird, "Images of Women," 54.

13. Sheila Briggs, "Galatians," in Elisabeth Schüssler Fiorenza, *Searching the Scriptures: A Feminist Commentary* (New York: Crossroad, 1994), vol. 2, 218–36; 232.

14. Judith Romney Wegner discusses Torah prescriptions and rabbinic exemptions for women in *Chattel or Person? The Status of Women in the Mishnah* (New York: Oxford University Press, 1988), 6, 10–13, 146–47, 150–51. See p. 4 for Wegner's description of the ideal and prescriptive perspective of the Mishnah. Jewish women were not obligated to meet the requirements of time-bound laws, given that performance of them would interfere with obligations in the home. Relief of obligation is not a gift but an exclusion. It creates a gulf between public and private spheres. Women were denied the obligation — privilege — of the study of the law, excluding them from an important dimension of the religious cult and from public roles such as that of judge. See also, "Women," in Geoffrey Wigoder, ed., *The Encyclopedia of Judaism* (New York: Macmillan Publishing Co., 1989), 732–34; and Neusner, "Women in the System of the Mishnah," 9. As Neusner points out, the tractates of the Mishnah are "remote from everyday life" (3); for example, one division is devoted to the Temple but there is no longer a Temple. Caution must be used in taking the literary sources in the tradition (Torah, Mishnah) as historical sources. A post-biblical writing, the Mishnah is dated usually in the late second century. H. L. Strack and G. Stemberger treat the complexity of its dating in *Introduction to the Talmud and Midrash* (Minneapolis: Fortress Press, 1992), 119–66.

15. Wegner, *Chattel or Person?* 147. On the Torah as authority, see p. 12.

16. Ibid., 150. On the ranking of Israelite women below male proselytes, see pp. 14–15.

17. James D. G. Dunn, *Jesus, Paul and the Law: Studies in Mark and Galatians* (Louisville: Westminster, 1990), 194. While it is true that full proselytes took on Jewish identity by their affiliation with the people of Israel and were obligated to keep Torah commands, their status was not without ambiguity. See Shaye J. D. Cohen, "Crossing the Boundary and Becoming a Jew," *Harvard Theological Review* 82 (1989), 13–33; and idem, "Conversion to Judaism in Historical Perspective: From Biblical Israel to Postbiblical Judaism," *Conservative Judaism* 36 (1983), 31–45. On women converts to Judaism, see H. H.

Rowley, *From Moses to Qumran: Studies in the Old Testament* (London: Lutterworth Press, 1963), 211–35.

18. Wayne A. Meeks, *The First Urban Christians: The Social World of the Apostle Paul* (New Haven: Yale University Press, 1983).

19. Bruce W. Winter, *Roman Wives, Roman Widows: The Appearance of New Women and the Pauline Communities* (Grand Rapids, Mich.: Eerdmans, 2003). On "new" Roman women whose sexual lives disrupted conventional norms, see pp. 21–31. The literary evidence is from contemporary writers, poets, and playwrights as well as the legislation formulated against such conduct by Augustus (22). Part I of Winter's study of Roman women sets the social context of women's participation in the Christian movement and the roles they took on within it; for example, the participation of Roman women in the public sphere contributed to the way in which women (such as those named in Romans 16) could contribute to Christian missionary activity in Corinth, Rome, and elsewhere (173). See, for example, the comparison of Junia Theodora and Phoebe (194–99).

20. The emperor Augustus found these activities so threatening that he created a new set of laws to counter them. He permanently banished his daughter Julia for her promiscuous behavior. She and her circle "operated on the extreme of the new Roman woman," says Winter, and, as the Roman biographer Suetonius recounts, "she did not neglect any act of extravagance or lust." Winter, *Roman Wives*, 29. Some upper-class married women even registered and operated as prostitutes, thus identifying with a class exempt from Augustus's legislation.

21. Karen Jo Torjesen, "Reconstruction of Women's Early Christian History," in Elisabeth Schüssler Fiorenza, *Searching the Scriptures: A Feminist Introduction* (New York: Crossroad, 1993), vol. 1, 290–310; 304.

22. Winter, *Roman Wives*, 38.

23. Winters, *Roman Wives*, 182. On women and the courts, see pp. 174–79. Carfania is discussed on p. 177, Phile on p. 181, and Junia Theodora on pp. 183–91. Historian J. Rive points to the significance of inscriptions: "The importance of women in civic life is another aspect of the ancient world that is known almost entirely from inscriptions, since literary and legal sources depict women as largely

relegated to private life" (181). Official inscriptions provide a record of the public offices held by women.

24. Ibid., 175. Winter cites the important article by Jane Gardner, "Women in Business Life."

25. Meeks, *The First Urban Christians*, 24.

26. Elisabeth Schüssler Fiorenza notes the Jewish colony at Elephantine: *In Memory of Her: A Feminist Theological Reconstruction of Christian Origins* (New York: Crossroad, 1987), 109.

27. Meeks, *The First Urban Christians*, 23; citing Diogenes Laërtius 6.12, 7.175.

28. Winter, *Roman Wives*, 62. On the study of virtue, the qualities of a good wife, and implications for her husband, see pp. 63–65. The detractors' view is given on p. 67. Winter notes, too, that Cleanthes (d. 231 B.C.E.) and Diogenes Laërtius (fl. early third-century) held that virtue was the same for men and women. Seneca also believed that women were equal to men (*Ad Marciam* 16.1). Winter refers to C. E. Manning, "Seneca and Stoics on the Equality of the Sexes," *Mnemosyne Ser.* 4, 26 (1973), 170–77.

29. Ibid. See pp. 66–68 on educating daughters. For Musonius's views of equality in sex and marriage, see 70–71.

30. Ibid., 114. Winter notes that the *symposia* and dinner parties were held in homes, the same setting for meetings of the early church. He notes Paul's expressed concerns about women's behavior and disorder in the community's worship in 1 Corinthians 11–14 are similar to discussions about women in philosophical treatises (115).

31. Ibid., 14. Juvenal, *Satires*, 6.448–56.

32. Torjesen, "Reconstruction" on Greek and Roman women. I draw here from pp. 294–95.

33. Ibid., 295.

34. Meeks, *First Urban Christians*, 25.

35. Ilan, *Integrating Women*, 37. On the emergence and development of rabbinic power after the Jewish-Roman War (67–70 C.E.), see Howard Clark Kee, Eric M. Meyers, John Rogerson, and Anthony J. Saldarini, eds., *The Cambridge Companion to the Bible* (Cambridge: Cambridge University Press, 1997), 419–21.

36. Kraemer, *Blessings*, 93.

37. Schüssler Fiorenza, *In Memory of Her*, 108–9.

38. On the first-century synagogue, see Howard Clark Kee, "Defining the First-Century C.E. Synagogue: Problems and Progress," in Howard Clark Kee and Lynn H. Cohick, eds., *Evolution of the Synagogue: Problems and Progress* (Harrisburg, Pa.: Trinity Press International, 1999), 7–26. The image of a synagogue as a building reflects second- and third-century developments. The word "synagōge" meant assembly, gathering, community, and "synaga" meant "to bring together." First-century synagogues, Kee argues, are just that — gatherings serving social, political, military, and religious purposes. A social and religious institution rather than a physical structure, the gathering takes place in private households — so, too, the Christian *ekklēsia*.

39. See Bernadette Brooten, *Women Leaders in the Ancient Synagogue*, Brown Judaic Studies 36 (Atlanta: Scholars Press, 1982), 150; and Shaye Cohen, "Women in the Synagogues of Antiquity," *Conservative Judaism* 34 (1980), 23–29; 24–25.

40. See Tessa Rajak and David Noy, "*Archisynagōgoi*: Office, Title and Social Status in the Greco-Roman Synagogue," *Journal of Religious Studies* 83 (1993), 75–93. I am grateful to Carolyn Osiek for this source.

41. Cohen, "Women," 24–25. The following example of the Therapeutae and Therapeutrides is given in Schüssler Fiorenza, *In Memory of Her*, 215–16.

42. Ekkehard W. Stegemann and Wolfgang Stegemann, *The Jesus Movement: A Social History of Its First Century* (Minneapolis: Fortress Press, 1999), 257. On women converts to Judaism, see, for example, Rowley, *From Moses to Qumran*, 211–35; Brooten, *Women Leaders*, 144–47; Cohen, "Conversion to Judaism," 31–45; idem, "Crossing," 13–33; Kraemer, *Blessings*, 106, 121–23; and Judith M. Lieu, "The 'Attraction of Women' in/to Early Judaism and Christianity: Gender and the Politics of Conversion," *Journal for the Study of the New Testament* 72 (1998), 16–19.

43. Louis H. Feldman, "Jewish Proselytism," in Harold W. Attridge and Gohei Hata, eds., *Eusebius, Christianity, and Judaism* (Detroit: Wayne State University Press, 1992), 372–408; 376; 407. Synonymous with Asia Minor, Anatolia has several regions, among which were Northern and Southern Galatia. On women Feldman cites

A. T. Kraabel, "Judaism in Western Asia Minor under the Roman Empire, with a Preliminary Study of the Jewish Community of Sardis, Lydia," 149–54. Harvard Ph.D. dissertation, 1998.

44. Brooten, *Women Leaders*, 146.

45. Feldman, "Jewish Proselytism," 393. Also Mary C. Boys, *Has God Only One Blessing? Judaism as a Source of Christian Self-Understanding* (New York: Paulist Press, 2000), 55–56.

46. Citing *Cicero* vii.6 and *Josephus*, War ii. 463, James Dunn says that it is well attested that many Gentiles adopted Jewish customs and attended Jewish synagogues. Dunn, *Galatians*, 129; and idem, *The Parting of the Ways*, 125–33.

47. Alan F. Segal, *Rebecca's Children: Judaism and Christianity in the Roman World* (Cambridge, Mass.: Harvard University Press, 1986), 98. Segal discusses this more extensively in *Paul the Convert: The Apostolate and Apostasy of Saul the Pharisee* (New Haven: Yale University Press, 1990), 117–49.

48. Stegemann and Stegemann, *The Jesus Movement*, 389.

49. Stephen J. Patterson, "Paul and the Jesus Tradition: It Is Time for Another Look," *Harvard Theological Review* 84:1 (January 1991), 23–42; 33–35.

50. Margaret Y. MacDonald, "Was Celsus Right? The Role of Women in the Expansion of Early Christianity," in David L. Balch and Carolyn Osiek, *Early Christian Families in Context: An Interdisciplinary Dialogue* (Eerdmans, 2003), 157–84, 158.

51. See Schüssler Fiorenza, "The Early Christian Movement: Equality in the Power of the Spirit," *In Memory of Her*, 160–204.

52. Elizabeth A. Castelli discusses the titles, the authenticity of Rom. 16, and its placement in "Romans," in Elisabeth Schüssler Fiorenza, ed., *Searching the Scriptures*, vol. 2, 276–80. Castelli considers Rom. 16 "an integral part of the larger text of Romans" (276).

53. Ibid., 278–79.

54. Stegemann and Stegemann, *The Jesus Movement*, 280. See pp. 397 for the descriptive phrase, "indifference to gender" below.

55. "Paul held that faith in Jesus now defined the circle of those whom God accepts..." Hurtado, *Lord Jesus Christ: Devotion to Jesus in Earliest Christianity* (Grand Rapids, Mich.: Eerdmans, 2003), 89.

56. As noted in chapter 1, the phrase the "truth of the gospel" means for Paul that Gentiles *as Gentiles* now have equal access to

salvation — covenant membership — and are no longer required to become Jews for this access, a position Paul believed was validated by the Gentiles' reception of God's Spirit on the basis of their faith. See Sanders, *Paul and Palestinian Judaism*, 457–58. The idea is central to Paul's thought and routinely discussed. See, for example, Hans Dieter Betz, *Galatians*, Hermeneia (Philadelphia: Fortress Press, 1979), 28–29; Dunn, *Galatians*, 127; and Roetzel, *Paul: The Man and the Myth* (Minneapolis: Fortress Press, 1999), 121–25.

57. James D. G. Dunn, *Jesus and the Spirit: A Study of Religious and Charismatic Experience of Jesus and the First Christians as Reflected in the New Testament* (London: SCM Press, 1975; reprinted 1997, Eerdmans.), 260. On the corporate dimension of religious experience, see esp. ch. 9, "The Body of Christ — The Consciousness of Community," 259–300. The points that follow here are drawn from pp. 260–63 in particular.

58. Larry W. Hurtado, *Lord Jesus Christ*, 106 n. 67.

59. Stegemann and Stegemann, *The Jesus Movement*, 397.

60. Krister Stendahl, *The Bible and the Role of Women*, trans. Emilie T. Sander (Philadelphia: Fortress Press, 1966), 32.

61. Ibid., 33; emphasis added.

62. Peter Lampe, "The Language of Equality in Early Christian House Churches: A Constructivist Approach," in Balch and Osiek, eds., *Early Christian Families in Context*, 73–83; 78.

63. Krister Stendahl, "A Response," *Union Seminary Quarterly Review* 33 (1978), 189–91; 189.

64. Brooten, *Women Leaders*, 150. See also Ilan, *Integrating Women*, 33.

65. Schüssler Fiorenza, *In Memory of Her*, 106. See pp. 249–50 for a discussion of women in Asia Minor.

66. Meeks, *The First Urban Christians*, 25.

67. Kraemer, *Blessings*, 100.

68. See R. L. Wilken, "Judaism in Roman and Christian Society," *Journal of Religion* 47 (1967), 327–28.

69. Ibid., 390.

70. Recall Sanders's view that these presuppositions reflect systematic misunderstanding in the Christian tradition. Sanders, *Paul and Palestinian Judaism*, 233.

71. Roetzel, *Paul*, 122.

Chapter 5. Recovering Paul — and the Gospel

1. To argue that Galatians is in some way about women is not the usual reading of Galatians. Unlike most, Sheila Briggs takes up the subject of women in her commentary, "Galatians," in Elisabeth Schüssler Fiorenza, *Searching the Scriptures: A Feminist Commentary* (New York: Crossroad, 1994), vol. 2, 218–36. About the baptismal formula, Briggs writes, "There it is not embedded in an argument for women's equality but serves Paul's predominant interest, namely, to show the incompatibility of observance of the law with faithfulness to the Christian gospel" (220).

2. Elisabeth Schüssler Fiorenza, "Women in the Pre-Pauline and Pauline Churches," *Union Seminary Quarterly Review* 33 (1978), 153–66; 155.

3. Phyllis Bird, "Images of Women in the Old Testament," in Rosemary Radford Ruether, *Religion and Sexism: Images of Women in the Jewish and Christian Traditions* (New York: Simon and Schuster, 1974), 41–88; 41.

4. On androcentric texts and historical reality, see Elisabeth Schüssler Fiorenza, *Discipleship of Equals: A Feminist Ekklesialogy of Liberation* (New York: Crossroad, 1993), 41–60.

5. Elisabeth Schüssler Fiorenza, *Bread Not Stone: The Challenge of Feminist Biblical Interpretation* (Boston: Beacon Press, 1984), 112. See also pp. x–xi and 15–22.

6. See the brief historical survey by J. Christiaan Beker, *Paul the Apostle: The Triumph of God in Life and Thought* (Philadelphia: Fortress Press, 1980) from the work of Ferdinand Christian Baur (1831) through Ernst Käsemann (1971), 11–15. Beker writes that "Today it is widely recognized that Paul's thought cannot be grasped in terms of a systematic doctrinal core" (14). He then describes the many ways in his contemporaries at that time identified the core of Paul's thought. He identifies the "coherent center" of Paul's thought as "a symbolic structure in which a primordial experience (Paul's call) is brought into language in a particular way.... That language is, for Paul, the apocalyptic language of Judaism, in which he lived and thought" (15–16).

7. Ibid., 340. These judgments, says Beker, are identified as those of Julius Wellhausen and a "popular line of interpreting Judaism

that was widespread in the so-called Weber-Bousset-Schürer line of scholarship and that perverted many generations of Christian scholarship on Judaism." Beker notes that it is one of the great merits of E. P. Sanders's *Paul and Palestinian Judaism* that "he destroyed this anti-Jewish bias in scholarship once and for all" (340). This was certainly in accord with Sanders's own purpose. A chance listening to an evangelical radio show focusing on Paul and the law indicates that Beker's judgment is, unfortunately, optimistic and that not everyone has read or agreed with Sanders.

8. Peter Borgen, *Early Christianity and Hellenistic Judaism* (Edinburgh: T & T Clark, 1996), 257. Borgen identifies this view with H. Schlier. It is a view "pointedly formulated in the Reformation, and is today followed by scholars such as Bultmann..." (257).

9. Carolyn Osiek, "Philippians," in Schüssler Fiorenza, *Searching the Scriptures*, vol. 2, 237–49; 237.

10. Elisabeth Schüssler Fiorenza, *Bread Not Stone: The Challenge of Feminist Biblical Interpretation* (Boston: Beacon Press, 1984), 112. The following point is from p. 112 as well.

11. Hans Dieter Betz, *Galatians*, Hermeneia (Philadelphia: Fortress Press, 1979), 28.

12. Larry W. Hurtado, *Lord Jesus Christ: Devotion to Jesus in Earliest Christianity* (Grand Rapids, Mich.: Eerdmans, 2003), 164.

13. Betz, *Galatians*, 8–9. Emphasis added.

14. Frank J. Matera, "Galatians in Perspective," *Interpretation* 54/3 (2000), 233–45; 24. Emphasis added.

15. Betz, *Galatians*, 3.

16. Elisabeth Schüssler Fiorenza, *In Memory of Her: A Feminist Theological Reconstruction of Christian Origins* (New York: Crossroad, 1987), 210.

17. Ibid., 217.

18. Ibid., 217–18.

19. Alan F. Segal, *Rebecca's Children: Judaism and Christianity in the Roman World* (Cambridge, Mass.: Harvard University Press, 1986), 115.

20. John M. G. Barclay, *Obeying the Truth: Paul's Ethics in Galatians* (Minneapolis: Fortress Press, 1988), 58–60.

21. Ibid., 60.

22. Pheme Perkins, *Gnosticism and the New Testament* (Minneapolis: Fortress Press, 1993), 166.

23. Schüssler Fiorenza, *In Memory of Her*, 183.

24. Wayne A. Meeks, *The Moral World of the First Christians* (Philadelphia: Westminster Press, 1986), 126.

25. Ross Shepard Kraemer, *Her Share of the Blessings: Women's Religions among Pagans, Jews, and Christians in the Greco-Roman World* (New York: Oxford University Press, 1992), 93. Also Louis H. Feldman, "Jewish Proselytism," in Harold W. Attridge and Gohei Hata, eds., *Eusebius, Christianity, and Judaism* (Detroit: Wayne State University Press, 1992), 372–408; 376; and Bernadette Brooten, *Women Leaders in the Ancient Synagogue*, Brown Judaic Studies 36 (Atlanta: Scholars Press, 1982).

26. Betz, *Galatians*, 7. Similarly, James D. G. Dunn, *The Epistle to the Galatians*, Black's New Testament Commentary (Peabody, Mass.: Hendrickson, 1993), 9–11.

27. John Painter, *Just James: The Brother of Jesus in History and Tradition* (Minneapolis: Fortress Press, 1999), 56.

28. Torah prescriptions for women and rabbinic exemptions are discussed in Judith Romney Wegner, *Chattel or Person? The Status of Women in the Mishnah* (New York: Oxford University Press, 1988), 6, 10–13, 150–51, 146–47. The complexity of dating and of using the Mishnah as a historical source for the first-century has been noted.

29. Ross Shepard Kraemer ed., *Maenads, Martyrs, Matrons, and Monastics: A Sourcebook on Women's Religions in the Greco-Roman World* (Philadelphia: Fortress Press, 1988), 175.

30. Ibid., 301.

31. Kraemer, *Blessings*, 100.

32. Alan F. Segal, *Paul the Convert: The Apostolate and Apostasy of Saul the Pharisee* (New Haven: Yale University Press, 1990), 121–22.

33. 1 Timothy 2:8–15.

INDEX